The law of cabs in London : including motor cabs : with appendices containing police notices, the Asquith award, and the text of the statutes arranged both as a legal treatise and a popular handbook.

Herman Cohen

The law of cabs in London : including motor cabs : with appendices containing police notices, the Asquith award, and the text of the statutes arranged both as a legal treatise and a popular handbook.
Cohen, Herman
collection ID ocm32767325
Reproduction from Columbia Law School Library
Includes index.
London : Jordan & Sons, 1899.
vii, 163 p. ; 19 cm.

The Making of Modern Law collection of legal archives constitutes a genuine revolution in historical legal research because it opens up a wealth of rare and previously inaccessible sources in legal, constitutional, administrative, political, cultural, intellectual, and social history. This unique collection consists of three extensive archives that provide insight into more than 300 years of American and British history. These collections include:

Legal Treatises, 1800-1926: over 20,000 legal treatises provide a comprehensive collection in legal history, business and economics, politics and government.

Trials, 1600-1926: nearly 10,000 titles reveal the drama of famous, infamous, and obscure courtroom cases in America and the British Empire across three centuries.

Primary Sources, 1620-1926: includes reports, statutes and regulations in American history, including early state codes, municipal ordinances, constitutional conventions and compilations, and law dictionaries.

These archives provide a unique research tool for tracking the development of our modern legal system and how it has affected our culture, government, business – nearly every aspect of our everyday life. For the first time, these high-quality digital scans of original works are available via print-on-demand, making them readily accessible to libraries, students, independent scholars, and readers of all ages.

The BiblioLife Network

This project was made possible in part by the BiblioLife Network (BLN), a project aimed at addressing some of the huge challenges facing book preservationists around the world. The BLN includes libraries, library networks, archives, subject matter experts, online communities and library service providers. We believe every book ever published should be available as a high-quality print reproduction; printed on-demand anywhere in the world. This insures the ongoing accessibility of the content and helps generate sustainable revenue for the libraries and organizations that work to preserve these important materials.

The following book is in the "public domain" and represents an authentic reproduction of the text as printed by the original publisher. While we have attempted to accurately maintain the integrity of the original work, there are sometimes problems with the original work or the micro-film from which the books were digitized. This can result in minor errors in reproduction. Possible imperfections include missing and blurred pages, poor pictures, markings and other reproduction issues beyond our control. Because this work is culturally important, we have made it available as part of our commitment to protecting, preserving, and promoting the world's literature.

GUIDE TO FOLD-OUTS MAPS and OVERSIZED IMAGES

The book you are reading was digitized from microfilm captured over the past thirty to forty years. Years after the creation of the original microfilm, the book was converted to digital files and made available in an online database.

In an online database, page images do not need to conform to the size restrictions found in a printed book. When converting these images back into a printed bound book, the page sizes are standardized in ways that maintain the detail of the original. For large images, such as fold-out maps, the original page image is split into two or more pages

Guidelines used to determine how to split the page image follows:

- Some images are split vertically; large images require vertical and horizontal splits.
- For horizontal splits, the content is split left to right.
- For vertical splits, the content is split from top to bottom.
- For both vertical and horizontal splits, the image is processed from top left to bottom right.

THE LAW OF CABS

IN

LONDON

(INCLUDING MOTOR CABS)

THE LAW OF CABS IN LONDON

(INCLUDING MOTOR CABS)

WITH

APPENDICES CONTAINING POLICE NOTICES, THE ASQUITH AWARD, AND THE TEXT OF THE STATUTES

Arranged both as a Legal Treatise and a Popular Handbook

BY

HERMAN COHEN

OF THE INNER TEMPLE, BARRISTER-AT-LAW

JORDAN & SONS, LIMITED

120 CHANCERY LANE, AND 8 BELL YARD, LONDON, W.C.

1899

Spec. Law C
20-46101

Law Library

PRINTED BY
JORDAN AND SONS, LIMITED, 120 CHANCERY LANE,
LONDON, W.C.

PREFACE.

THE excuse for bringing out this little volume is that there does not exist, and never has existed, any book exclusively devoted to its subject. I am not aware that any comment has yet appeared upon the Act of 1896.

In preparing the following pages I have made much use of the relevant section in *Archibald's Metropolitan Police Guide*, 1896.

I have to thank the authorities of New Scotland Yard, and especially Inspector DORMER, and the Secretary of the London Cabdrivers' Union for much useful information. I have also to thank my friend Mr. J. G. PEASE, of the Inner Temple, for reading the proof sheets and for many valuable suggestions.

It has been part of my scheme to print the passages chiefly designed for the lay reader in bolder type than the strictly legal portions of the book.

The notation used in citing Statutes is less cumbrous than that usually adopted (*e.g.* 40-1 V. 60, 3, instead of 40-41 Vict. cap. 60, sec. 3), but, it is hoped, is perfectly plain.

The Index has been prepared with a view to practical use rather than to literary form.

HERMAN COHEN.

THE TEMPLE,
Easter, 1899.

TABLE OF CONTENTS.

	PAGES
Table of Cases Cited	viii
Introduction	1–7
Definition of a Cab	9–11
Motors	9, 10
London, Meaning of	11, 12
Plying for Hire	13–16
The Right to Hire	16–26
Railway Cabs	19–25
Cabs to Railways	25–26
Inability to Pay	26
Infectious Diseases	26
Fare Beforehand	27
Remedies of both Parties	28–51
Remedies of the Hirer	28–44
Overcharge	29–32
Penalties	32–35
„ List of	36–43
Compensation	44
Remedies of the Driver	45–51
„ „ against Proprietors	51
Fares	52–56
Limitations of Hiring	57
Fares when Driver not bound to go	57
Sunday	58
Cabmen as Messengers or Carriers	58
Other Payments	58
Children	58
Speed	61

	PAGES
Luggage	61–63
Lighting	64–66
Loss, Injury, or Damage through Negligence	66–74
Relations between the Authorities and Proprietors and Drivers	74–89
1 Proprietors	74–81
2 Drivers	82–85
3 Relations between Drivers and Proprietors	85–89
Procedure	90, 91
Appeal	91
Places in Metropolitan Police District not in Middlesex—Appendix A	92, 93
Police Notice to Drivers of Hansoms—Appendix B	94
" " " Proprietors—Appendix C	95, 96
" " as to Motors—Appendix D	97–103
Asquith Award—Appendix E.	104, 105
Hackney Carriage Statutes	106–154
The London Hackney Carriage Act, 1831	106–117
The London Hackney Carriages Act, 1843	118–137
The London Hackney Carriages Act, 1850	138–139
The London Hackney Carriages Act, 1853	140–146
The London Hackney Carriages Act, 1853	147–148
The Metropolitan Carriage Act, 1869	149–153
The London Cab Act, 1896	154
Index	155–163

TABLE OF CASES CITED.

Allen v Tunbridge, 15
Anderson v Wood, 42

Bateson v Oddy, 11
Bocking v Jones, 53
Brind v Dale, 66

Case v Storey, 19
Clark v Stanford, 15
Cloud v Turfery, 90
Commissioners of Police v. Reg, 83
Coupé Company v Maddick, 74
Curtis v Embery, 14

Dyke v Elliott, 24

Engelhart v Farren, 70

Fornett v Clark, 23
Foulger v Steadman, 24.
Fowler v Lock, 68

Heather v Brewer, 89
Hodges v The London Tramways and Omnibus Co., 76
Hole v Digby, 25
Hudston v Midland Railway Co, 63
Hurrell v Ellis, 88

Keen v Henry, 73
Kerswill v Reg, 47.
King v London Improved Cab Co, Limited, 72

King v. Spurr, 70
Kippins, *ex parte*, 26

Mann v Ward, 70
Marriott v London and South-Western Railway Co, 25
Milson v. Silvester, 68
Morley v Dunscombe, 68

Norris v Birch, 87
Norton v Jones, 60

O'Neil v City and County Finance Co., 81.
Ord v Gemmell & Son, Limited, 67

Painter, *ex parte*, 25
Perth General Station Committee v Ross, 25
Powles v Hider, 67

Reg v Commissioners of Police, 83
Reg v Kerswill, 47.
Rogers v Macnamara, 88.
Ross v. Hill, 66

Skinner v Usher, 13

Venables v. Smith, 70

Warren v. Wildee, 69
Wright v. London General Omnibus Co., 44

INTRODUCTION.

"IN the reign of Elizabeth," says a writer in Traill's *Social England* (vol. 3, p. 397), "all long journeys were performed on horseback; no kind of light carriage existed. Royal personages possessed lumbering gilt coaches, but towards the end of the reign coaches were beginning to be used by the wealthy in the London streets." These, of course, were private vehicles, and their appearance in the streets was resented by the carmen, who nicknamed them "hell-carts," probably on account of the space they took up (*ibid*, vol 4, p 324).

Hackney Carriages were (according to the *Encyclopædia Britannica*, Edn. 9, Art. "Carriages") first established in London in 1625 "On the 1st of April, 1639 [1634 in *Encycl. Brit.*]," says the *Book of Days* (vol. 1, p. 459), "Mr. Garrard, writing in London to Wentworth, Earl of Strafford, then Lord Lieutenant of Ireland, says. 'I cannot omit to mention any new thing that comes up amongst us, though never so trivial Here is one Captain Baily; he hath been a sea-captain, but now lives on the land about this city, where he tries experiments, he hath erected, according to his ability, some four hackney-coaches, put his men in a livery, and appointed them to stand at the Maypole in the Strand, giving them instructions at what rate to carry men into several parts of the town, where all day they may be had. Other hackney men seeing this way, they flocked to the same place, and performed their journeys at the same rate, so that sometimes there is twenty of them together, which disperse up and down, that they and others are to be had everywhere, as watermen are to be had by the water-side. Everybody is much pleased with it; for, whereas before coaches could not be had but at greater rates, now a man may have one much cheaper.'"

Roundly then, we may fix the date of the introduction of these vehicles into the metropolis at about 1600. They steadily grew in favour, for in 1637 it is asserted that there were fifty in London and Westminster. The rate of increase may be gathered from the following passage:—

"The seventh branch," says Blackstone in his great work in 1765, "of the extraordinary perpetual revenue [of the Crown] is the duty arising from licences to hackney coaches and chairs in London, and the parts adjacent. In 1654 200 hackney coaches were allowed within London, Westminster, and six miles round, under the direction of the Court of Aldermen (*Scobell*, 313). By statute 13 & 14 Car. II. c. 2 400 were licensed, and the money arising thereby was applied to repairing the streets (*Com. Journ.*, 14th February, 1661). This number was increased to 700 by statute 5 W. & M. c. 22 and the duties vested in the Crown, and by the statute 9 Anne c. 23 and other subsequent statutes (10 Anne c. 19 s. 158, 12 Geo. I c. 15, 33 Geo. II. c. 25) there are now 800 licensed coaches and 400 chairs. This revenue is governed by Commissioners of its own, and is, in truth, a benefit to the subject, as the expense of it is felt by no individual, and its necessary regulations have established a competent jurisdiction, whereby a very refractory race of men may be kept in some tolerable order" (Book I. c. 8, p. 327)

At first, the new vehicles met with opposition from tradesmen, watermen, and others, who supposed that their vested interests were hurt; and the manners of the times are well illustrated by the views of such folk on the subject, as later by the opposition of the coachmen, in their turn, to such an innovation as the umbrella. Thus Taylor, the "water poet," who flourished about 1630, is cited in the "Book of Days" (*ubi supra*) as writing: "A coach, like a heathen, a pagan, an infidel, or an atheist, observes neither Sabbath nor holiday, time nor season, robustiously breaking through the toil or net of divine and human law, order, and authority, and, as it were, condemning all Christian conformity, like a dog that lies on a heap of hay, who will eat none of it himself nor suffer any other beast to eat any. Even so, the coach is not capable of hearing what a preacher saith, nor will it suffer men or women to hear that would hear, for it makes such a hideous rumbling in the streets by many church doors that people's ears are stopped with the noise, whereby they are debarred of their edifying, which makes faith so fruitless, good works so barren, and charity as cold at Midsummer as if it were a great frost, and by this means souls are robbed and starved of their heavenly manna, and the kingdom of darkness replenished. To avoid which they have set up a cross-post in Cheapside on Sundays, near Wood Street end, which makes the coaches rattle and jumble on the other side of the way, further from the church and from hindering of their hearing."

In the *Encyclopædia Britannica* it is stated that the hackney coach held its place till 1820, when the "cab" from Paris supplanted it, and that Mr. Hansom patented his now familiar invention[1] in 1834.

"Down to 1814," says Mr. Dowell in his *History of Taxation in England*, "the Londoner could only call a 'coach' to carry four persons inside and a servant on the outside, but in that year hackney chariots to carry two inside and a servant outside were introduced, and 200 were admitted to license as part of the 1100 hackney carriages allowed under the existing law. Such was the utility and convenience of these hackney chariots that in the next year the number was doubled, and the number of persons to be carried was extended to three 'insides' —thus introducing the 'Bodkin' of the 'diligence'—and a servant outside. Moreover, permission was given to the Commissioners to license such a number as the Treasury ordered of carriages lighter even than the chariot in construction, on two wheels and drawn by a single horse." These latter seem to have been first called "Cabs."

---

[1] "The modern so-called hansom cabs retain but few of the original ideas."— *Dict Nat Biog*, Art "Hansom." "'Tis the gondola of London," says Lothair of a "cruising hansom" (*Lothair*, c 27).

Serjeant Ballantine, speaking in his *Experiences* of London of about 1830, says, "A machine called a 'hackney coach,' licensed to carry six people, redolent of damp straw, driven by a still damper coachman, was the principal mode of locomotion. Omnibuses were unknown There sprang up, however, in my comparatively early days, a dissipated looking vehicle called a 'cab'. It was formed of an open box placed upon two high wheels. This was for the passenger, the driver sat upon a board by the side They were considered fast—not so much in motion as in character. However, the necessity for locomotion does away with prejudice, and I have lived to see an Archbishop in a hansom cab." This description of the vehicle, by the way, explains how Mr. Pickwick could carry on his famous conversation with the driver during the journey. Such an unfavourable reference to the manners of the drivers is by no means isolated in the literature of fiction in the first half of the century; and earlier, Blackstone, as we have seen, is not more complimentary.

As late as 1867 Sir (then Mr.) W. T. Charley (afterwards Q.C. and Common Serjeant of the City of London) wrote "The frequent recurrence of this offence [wilful misbehaviour causing hurt to person[1] or property] in the police reports shows how frightfully common it must be in the crowded thoroughfares of London. A mad bull is less dangerous than a cabman 'the worse for liquor,' raging like a demon along

---

[1] *Cf* Mr Sam Weller's epigram "two mile o' danger at eightpence" (c 22).

the streets, with the reins lying on the horse's back, at the rate of twelve, fifteen, or twenty miles an hour, now knocking down a woman 'walking on the pavement' and 'dragging her some distance,' now overturning another cab and throwing the passengers into the road, then finally plunging one of his own shafts through the panel of another cab or into the side of a cab-horse," and for every one of these incidents he gives chapter and verse (*The Law of London Cabs and Omnibuses*, pp 113-4)

It is now common knowledge that comparatively few such offences are committed. Indeed, there is no more convincing testimony to the improvement in cabmen as a class than the fact that, notwithstanding the great increase in their numbers, there are certainly relatively and probably absolutely fewer cases in which they figure in the police courts than at the time when Mr. Charley wrote. One consequence of this is that earlier years supply the most magistrates' decisions When the statutes were newer they were not so well understood, the law was less settled, and, perhaps, not so equitable to cabmen as in recent years.

As the industry grew legislation concerning it increased In the Act of 1831, no less than twenty-six statutes dealing with these vehicles are enumerated, of which the first is 9 Anne c 23, passed in 1710. New laws were sometimes (*e g.* in 1853 and 1867) followed by strikes, but this form of ventilating grievances was by no means reserved for such occasions. "Cab strikes were occurring every three years," said a member in the House of Commons on 25th May, 1894, during a debate on a strike then in progress. Out of that debate (in which it was stated that there were 15,000 licensed cab-drivers), sprang the Committee of Enquiry appointed by the Home Secretary in 1894, to the Minutes of Evidence before whom and to whose Report frequent reference is made in the following pages[1] They reported that in 1893 11,000 cabs were licensed, and that in 1870 there were 7,000

In 1897 (the latest year for which figures are available), 13,673 drivers, of whom 24 were for "motors," and 11,508 cabs, of which 18 were "motors" and 7,925 two-wheeled, were licensed

The great cab strike of 1896 is still fresh in the public memory.

The word "cab" does not occur in a statute till the Act of 1896 (s 3). It is a colloquial abbreviation of *cabriolet*: compare '*bus*. "*Capriole*, gambols of goat *Ces voitures sautent beaucoup*," is Mr. Dowell's amusing note (*ubi supra*, vol 3, p. 44).

The word "hackney," of which "hack" is an abbreviation, is apparently derived from an old French word for a sort of horse, and has nothing to do with the place name.

---

[1] The Minutes of Evidence and the Report (signed 2nd January, 1895) are contained in two volumes on the Cab Service of the Metropolis, separately published in 1895 by Messrs Eyre & Spottiswoode (C 7607 1 and C 7607) The former is cited in this book as "the Blue Book," and the latter as "the Report."

THE LAW OF CABS IN LONDON.

WHAT IS A CAB?

THE familiar Cab is known to the law as a Hackney Carriage (see Introduction). For the little legal distinction there is between a four-wheeler and a hansom see pp. 56, 59.

There is no reason in law why cabs should not be constructed to carry only one passenger, or more than four passengers inside, or why they should not be drawn by more than one horse.

See 1-2 W IV 22, 4, and a dictum of Kelly, C B, in *Case v Storey* (L R, 4 Ex 322) Such regulations as are in force with regard to the physical conditions of cabs will be found in Appendix C

It may be noticed that there is no legal restriction as to the kind of (tame) animal which draws the cab.

MOTOR CABS.

Motor Cabs—"light locomotives" in the eyes of the law—are subject to the general law of Cabs, so far as it can be applied (practically, that is, entirely with the exception of any part of it specially relating to horses), and are, besides, subject to a special statute and special regulations.

The statute is The Locomotives on Highways Act, 1896 (59-60 V. 36). The regulations of the Local Government Board under that Act are printed in Appendix D. On this subject generally see *Bonner on Motor Cars*, p 6 *et seq*

A Police Notice, in advertising those regulations, adds—

"By Section 1 of the above-mentioned Act a light locomotive is to be deemed to be a carriage within the meaning of any Act of Parliament, whether public, general or local, and of any rule, regulation, or bye-law made under any Act of Parliament, and if used as a carriage of any particular class is to be deemed to be a carriage of that class, and the law relating to carriages of that class is to apply accordingly Consequently, if, *e g*, a light locomotive is used as a hackney or stage carriage, all statutory provisions and orders with regard to hackney and stage carriages in force in the Metropolitan Police District will apply thereto, and in addition the whole of the various statutes relating to highways which deal with the regulation of vehicular traffic apply equally"

The same Notice further points out that persons using motor cabs are not *necessarily* entitled to drive at the maximum rate of speed laid down in the regulations, "but only at such a rate as is reasonable and proper, having regard to the traffic on the highway." The Metropolitan Police Act, 1839, it is added, applies to motor cabs In the Police Notice to Cab Proprietors two paragraphs (15, 16) now deal especially with motor cabs (see Appendix C).

It was expressly provided by 3-4 W IV 48, 7, that the Act of 1831 should only apply to carriages drawn or impelled by animal power

A cab in London means any carriage for the conveyance of passengers which plies for hire within the Metropolitan Police District or the City, and is not a stage carriage that is, practically not an omnibus or vehicle used as an omnibus, where each passenger is liable to pay a separate and distinct fare. Every cab is a hackney carriage, but not every hackney carriage is a cab: for instance, a donkey-chaise or a goat-chaise may be a hackney carriage. It may be that the "privileged omnibus" at a railway station is a hackney carriage (32-3 V. 115, 4, and see s 2).

There is a definition of "hackney carriage" 1-2 W. IV 22, 4, and another 6-7 V 86, 2, practically agreeing with the one above, and yet another for Revenue purposes 51-2 V 8, 4 (3)[1] See also 7 W IV & 1 V. 36, 8 In a non-London case (1874) a "hackney carriage" at common law was considered Blackburn, J, thought that "common hire is the test of a hackney carriage" (*Bateson v. Oddy*, 30 L. T, N S 712)

LONDON.

With regard to the words "in London," it is to be noted that the details of the Law of Cabs vary as between London and other places. What, then, does London include? First the City, then the Metropolitan Police District.

This was constituted by Parliament in 1829, and originally consisted of certain places enumerated in the Schedule to an Act. Under another Act in 1840 an Order in Council was made declaring a great many other places to be within the district, and since then the district has not been altered. Practically, all these places together make up the area of the County of Middlesex (always excluding the City) and of certain

---

[1] "Hackney carriage" means any carriage standing or plying for hire, and includes any carriage let for hire by a coachmaker or other person whose trade or business it is to sell carriages or to let carriages for hire, provided that such carriage is not let for a period amounting to three months or more

bordering parts of Herts, Essex, Kent, and Surrey which are fifteen miles (or thereabouts) distant from Charing Cross. London then, for present purposes, means the whole of this area, for it = the City and the Metropolitan Police District

This view of the Metropolitan Police District follows from 10 G IV 44, 4 and 34 and Schedule, and 2-3 V 47, 2, and the Order in Council of 3rd January, 1840 (*London Gazette*, 13th and 16th October, 1840)

There is no express authority for the statement that the whole of Middlesex is within the Metropolitan Police District, but in effect it is so. Conceivably there may be spots or districts within this area not enumerated in the lists mentioned. In that case, a cab plying at such a spot would not be subject to the law prevailing in London, but the matter is of little practical importance

According to 2 3 V 47, 2, "any place which is part of the Central Criminal Court District, except the City of London and liberties thereof and also any part of any parish, township, precinct, or place which is not more than fifteen miles distant from Charing Cross in a straight line may be added to and form part of the Metropolitan Police District." The Central Criminal Court District was constituted in 1834 (by 4 5 W IV 36, 2), and included the County of Middlesex. Probably that county, *as such*, was not declared by the Order to be part of the Metropolitan Police District because it was not a "place" within the section just cited

The parishes and places in Middlesex, Essex, Kent, Surrey, and Herts now constituting this district are enumerated partly in the Schedule and partly in the Order [1]

Since 1840 any spot in the Metropolitan Police District is either in the County of Middlesex or within fifteen miles from Charing Cross "in a straight line"

Thus, the whole of Middlesex, with the exception of the City, is within the Metropolitan Police District, and the whole county is therefore, without any exception, under the London Cab Law

The Local Government Act of 1888 expressly left untouched the Metropolitan Police District (51-2 V. 41, 93 (1))

---

[1] For places in Essex, Kent, Surrey, and Herts see Appendix A

PLYING FOR HIRE.

What is "plying" or "plying for hire"? A cab is plying when it is standing still unhired where someone has the right to hire it. Thus, when it is standing in the master's yard it is not plying; and when it is plying, it may be plying for one class of hirers and not for another. It will be seen that the would-be hirer must have a legal right to be where the cab is (see pp 24, 25).

To "ply"=To work at steadily —*Skeat's Etymological Dictionary* I (4) To practise or perform with diligence and persistence, pursue steadily as, "to ply one's trade" II (6) To offer one's services for trips or jobs, as boatmen, hackmen, carriers, &c.—*Century Dictionary*

The definition above is suggested as on the whole the most practical. The phrase is illustrated by s 35 of the Act of 1831:—

"Every hackney carriage which shall be found standing in any street or place, and having thereon any of the numbered plates required by this Act to be fixed on hackney carriages, shall, unless actually hired, be deemed to be plying for hire, although such hackney carriage shall not be on any standing or place usually appropriated for the purpose of hackney carriages standing or plying for hire."

The section (20), referring to the "numbered plates," is repealed by 32-3 V 14, 39. It seems therefore that the words here alluding to them may be neglected

By 6-7 V. 86, 33, "every driver of a hackney carriage who shall ply for hire elsewhere than at some standing or place appointed for that purpose . . shall for every such offence forfeit the sum of twenty shillings" This creates the offence of "Crawling."

See also Penalty 15, p 38, *post* S 33 was considered in *Skinner v Usher* (L R, 7 Q B 423), 1872 There the question was whether a cab-driver who plied for hire on an open unenclosed piece of private ground, to which the public had access, but over which there was no public right of way, was within the section, but the Court of Queen's Bench (Blackburn, Hannen, and Quain, JJ) held that it was not. The plying for hire within this section must be in some public street or place.

Practically the same question came up in 1872 in *Curtis v Embery* (L R, 7 Ex 369)—not, however, a London case—and was decided in the same sense. "The reason of this legislation," said Bramwell, B, "is to protect the public who employ carriages plying for hire where there is nothing to control the condition of the carriages and the conduct of the driver but his own discretion. But there was no intention to protect them where the carriages and drivers are subject to the management of responsible persons, within whose private premises they stand to carry on the business."

Standings may only be in the centre of a street, unless the street has houses on one side only (6-7 V 86, 30). No cab may stand or ply opposite the General Post Office (7 W IV & 1 V 36, 8, and 6 7 V 86, 31), nor in or near Bloomsbury Square (13-4 V. 7, 6, saving 46 Geo III cxxxiv). Standings may be appointed and regulated by the Commissioners of Police (13-4 V 7 4) and they may appoint persons to enforce good order thereat (16-7 V 33, 12, 13). Such stands and such persons are subject to the regulations which the Secretary of State may make (32-3 V 115, 9 (2)), but in the City the consent of the Court of Lord Mayor and Aldermen must first be obtained to any stand so appointed (*Ibid*, Restriction 1).

Sir Godfrey Lushington, Permanent Under Secretary of State for the Home Department, stated to the Committee of Enquiry that he thought that "we have an arrangement with the Commissioner of Police that he is not to refuse a standing which is asked for by a Vestry, except he refers to the Secretary of State" (*Blue Book*, 9,238).

It is clear then that the law only contemplates cabs plying for hire by standing and waiting at certain defined spots (see p. 38).

It is to be noted that sometimes the statutes speak of "standing *and* plying" and sometimes of "standing *or* plying" (*e g* compare ss 5 and 35 of the Act of 1831).

In 32-3 V 115, 7, a distinction (in respect of the kind of standing) is clearly drawn in the case of an unlicensed cab between "plying for hire" and being "found on any stand," for there is a different penalty in each case. There can be no doubt that the distinction was introduced to meet such cases of plying as those at railway stations (see p 19).

The cases point the same way.

In *Bateson v Oddy* (30 L T, N S 712), a Harrogate case in 1874, alike in the arguments and the judgments it is assumed that the hackney carriage plying for hire "at common law" is standing somewhere. In other cases under the statutes the same assumption is made. See *Clarke v Stanford* (L R , 6 Q B 357), 1871, where Cockburn, C J , said "The case put by Mr Bosanquet of a carriage being on a man's own premises ready to go out if required is not what can be understood as 'plying for hire' within the meaning of this Act. But where a person has a carriage ready for the conveyance of passengers in a place frequented by the public he is plying for hire, although the place is private property." See also *Allen v Tunbridge* (L R., 6 C P 481), 1871, *Skinner v Usher* (L. R , 7 Q B 423), 1872, *Curtis v. Embery* (L R , 7 Ex 369), 1872, not a London case, and *Case v Storey* (L R., 4 Ex 319), 1869, where Channell, B , said "The intention" of s 35 of 1-2 W. IV 22 "doubtless was to prevent a cabdriver from capriciously refusing a fare *The common mode of doing so used to be by drawing off a stand, and then declining to allow the cab to be engaged*, and to prevent this mischief it was enacted" as in s 35 above. "But the street or place meant must be a street or place where both the driver and hirer may lawfully be." The words in italics clearly show that once the driver was "on the move" he was not plying for hire. The Act makes him so ply when he is accosted at a standstill.

There is apparently no case where it has been held or suggested that a cab in movement is plying for hire. But see a dictum of Channell, B , *obiter* in one report of *Case v. Storey* (38 L J , Mag Cases 117)

It by no means follows that any cab standing anywhere is at the beck and call of the first comer. It may be already engaged, and the driver may have a discretion as to whom he will take (see p 20). But, speaking generally, whenever an unhired cab is standing in any place in London, *in any sense public,* it is plying for hire. As to what places are public see p 24

As to an unlicensed cab plying for hire see p. 39. Of course, the driver of such a cab is not bound to take a fare

A cabdriver who plies elsewhere than at an appointed standing cannot make that an excuse for not taking a fare or otherwise complying with the law, unless he is actually a trespasser (as to which see p 24) A cabdriver not plying for hire may take a fare, and, if he does, in the absence of any special contract, he is bound by the same law as if he were plying for hire. As to special contracts see pp 19, 56, 57

THE RIGHT TO HIRE

A cabman plying for hire is bound, unless he is already engaged, to take, with few exceptions, any person who seeks to hire him If he refuses when properly asked he becomes liable to a penalty.

The Act of 1831 (s 35) says —

"The driver of every such hackney carriage [i.e plying for hire] which shall not be actually hired shall be obliged and compellable to go with any person desirous of hiring such hackney carriage, and upon the hearing of any complaint against the driver of any such hackney carriage for any such refusal, such driver shall be obliged to adduce evidence of having been and of being actually hired at the time of such refusal, and in case such driver shall fail to produce sufficient evidence of having been and of being so hired as aforesaid, he shall forfeit forty shillings" (see also s 36)

S 35 is still valid, but subject to the limitations mentioned above (p 15).

By 16-17 V 33, 7—

"The driver of every hackney carriage which shall ply for hire at any place within the limits of the Act shall (unless such driver have a reasonable excuse, to be allowed by the justice before whom the matter shall be brought in question) drive such hackney carriage to any place to which he shall be required by the hirer thereof to drive the same, not exceeding six miles from the place where the same shall have been hired, or for any time not exceeding one hour from the time when hired"

This applies to the whole London area (s 20)

What is "a reasonable excuse" in the words of the Act? Probably each case must be decided on its merits. But it may fairly be suggested that no magistrate would convict a cabman for refusing to take a drunk or a dirty person, or one whose mind was obviously disordered.

In a case at the Hammersmith Police Court reported in the *Times* of 17th July, 1865, the horse being tired was held to be a reasonable excuse.

May a cabman refuse to take an infant (*i.e.* a minor)?

Theoretically, Yes; but he would do so at his peril. It is no doubt quite easy to imagine cases—as, for instance, that of a street arab, who proposed to himself the treat of a free jaunt—where a justice would hold that there was a reasonable excuse for refusing. Other cases of would-be hirers obviously, presumably, or possibly unable to pay are dealt with below (see p. 26).

It is a general principle of law that an infant cannot bind himself by a contract, but there is a great exception for his benefit, that he may make a contract for "necessaries": and for these a cabman could, as usual, recover by suing. Now it would only be in the case of an "infant" of a very low social rank, if ever, that a cab would not be allowed to be a "necessary," and consequently a cabman's excuse on the ground of "infancy" would, in ninety cases out of a hundred, be considered frivolous by a magistrate. Occasionally, however, such a refusal might be valid.

"Necessaries," according to Wharton (*Law Lexicon*), is "a relative term, not strictly limited to such things as are absolutely requisite for support and subsistence, but to be construed literally, and varying with the state and degree, the rank, fortune, and age of the person to whom they are supplied."

"An article not *primâ facie* a necessary may become so under special circumstances, as a horse, or carriage exercise ordered by the doctor" (*Eversley, Domestic Relations*, 749)

Moreover, the cabman is specially protected by the "Bilking" Act of 1896 (59-60 V. 27), of which the chief section (1) runs:—

"1 If any person commits any of the following offences with respect to a cab namely—

(A) Hires a cab, knowing or having reason to believe that he cannot pay the lawful fare, or with intent to avoid payment of the lawful fare, or

(B) Fraudulently endeavours to avoid payment of a fare lawfully due from him, or

(C) Having failed or refused to pay a fare lawfully due from him, either refuses to give to the driver an address at which he can be found, or, with intent to deceive, gives a false address,

he shall be liable on summary conviction to pay, in addition to the lawful fare, a fine not exceeding forty shillings, or, in the discretion of the Court, to be imprisoned for a term not exceeding fourteen days, and the whole or any part of any fine imposed may be applied in compensation to the driver"

A nice question might arise whether infancy could ever be an answer to a cabman's claim or prosecution under this Act. It may be doubted whether the statute ever intended to touch the law of infancy, of which it is a general principle that a tradesman trusts an infant at his peril, and it might conceivably be argued that the phrases "lawful fare" and "lawfully due" prevent any relief under this Act where previously there was no civil remedy; if "infancy" is a good answer the section would not apply, for the fare would not be lawful, and if a cab was held to be a necessary it would apply As to the civil remedy see pp 46 to 48.

A married woman who hires a cab is deemed to contract with respect to and to bind her separate estate, unless the contrary is shown. She may be able to show that she contracted as her husband's agent, in which case he would be liable; and the question of fact must be decided on the circumstances of each case The only presumption in her favour is that if she is living with her husband she has authority to bind him for necessaries (45-6 V 75, 1 (2); 56-7 V. 63, 1, see p 17, *ante*), and even that presumption is limited.

"The cabman would expect payment from the person carried *unless a special contract to the contrary were entered into*," said a magistrate in a case (reported *Law Journal*, 10th Sep., 1887, p. 497) where a driver unsuccessfully sued a man for the fare for carrying his servant where the latter was "put into" the cab by the defendant's wife

RAILWAY CABS.

Practically the most important category of persons whom a cabman is not bound to take consists of those who have no legal right to be at the spot where he is plying. The only example worth considering is a cabstand at a railway station that is, on the private property of the railway company The right to hire such a cab is confined to passengers by the trains and to the railway officials The driver of such a cab is not bound to take non-passengers and persons who have no business at the station. Thus a person passing in the street has no right to turn into a railway station and take a cab, for the company might lawfully exclude him from their premises

The leading case on the subject is *Case v Storey* (L R, 4 Ex. 319, 38 L. J, M C 113, 20 L T 618, 17 W R 802) 1869 There the respondent had been admitted into the station with his cab by the railway company for the purpose of accommodating passengers arriving by their trains The station was the private property of the company The appellant, who had not on the occasion been a passenger by any train, but had entered the company's premises from the street, wanted to hire the respondent's cab, but the latter, upon learning that the appellant had not arrived by train, refused to take him. The appellant thereupon summoned the respondent (under 1-2 W. IV. 22, 35, 42, and 16-7 V. 33, 17), but the magistrate dismissed the summons, and the Court of Exchequer (Kelly, C.B., Bramwell, B., and Cleasby, B.) unanimously held that he was right.

"It is clear to me," said Kelly, C.B., "that railway stations are not either public streets or public roads. They are private property, and, although it is true they are places of public resort, that does not of itself make them public places. The public only resort there upon railway business, and the railway company might exclude them at any moment they like, except when a train was actually arriving or departing. For the proper carrying on of their business they must necessarily open their premises, which are nevertheless private, and in no possible manner capable of being described as public streets or roads. The decision at which I have arrived may possibly lead to some inconvenience to the public. If so, it will become the duty of the railway companies to obviate it by making proper regulations with the cabmen whom they authorise to enter their stations. The case really seems to me exactly analogous to that of an owner of a park permitting cabmen to come and stand within his grounds in order to accommodate his departing guests, and it could not be contended that, in that case, any passer-by might enter the park and insist on one of the cabmen there carrying him as a passenger."

"S. 35 of 1-2 W. IV. 22," said Bramwell, B., "is very inartificially drawn; but it cannot be meant to apply to a place to which the public have no right of access. Otherwise this absurd consequence might follow, that even in his master's yard he would be obliged to take anyone who chose to come into the yard and ask him."

"The street or place meant," said Channell, B., "must be a street or place where both the driver and hirer may lawfully be. Now here both elements are wanting. The cabman had no right to be on the railway company's premises. He was allowed to be there by the company for the accommodation of the public who might happen to be passengers by the trains. Then, again, the person who claimed to hire the respondent had no right to be on the railway premises at all."

Cleasby, B., also took this point, remarking (according to one report) "here the appellant was no better than a trespasser."—*W. R.*

All these judgments establish the proposition that a cabman at a stand in a railway station may refuse to take a non-passenger, but they also clearly imply that such a cabman must take a passenger.

According to one report the Chief Baron said —"The company allows cabs to come into the station before the arrival of the train, on the condition that they shall be hired only by persons coming by the train"—L T

The headnote in the *Law Journal* says —"The driver of a hackney carriage who, by arrangement with a railway company, is waiting in their station, using their private property, for any passenger arriving by train who may require to hire him is not liable to a penalty for refusing to be hired by a person not being such passenger" &c.

Nevertheless, some expressions of some of the learned judges imply that it was only by favour of the railway companies that passengers could use the cabs in stations, for they point out that, for any inconvenience the public (i.e passengers) might suffer in this behalf, the remedy lay in the companies making proper terms with the drivers to protect travellers

The question has never been expressly considered by a Court or in any other way, but it seems that the obligation on a railway cabman follows, as is implied rather than stated in the dicta of the learned judges just mentioned, from the former's contract with the companies, not from the latter's statutory right under any Hackney Carriage Act It is clear, if only from *Case v Storey* (and other cases), that such a cabman is on private property As Channell, B, says (*ubi supra*) "The cabman had no right to be on the company's premises He was allowed to be there by the company for the accommodation of the public who might happen to be passengers by the trains" And in the "exactly analogous" case put by the Chief Baron, could it be contended that one of the guests could compel the cabman to take him from private grounds (whatever the host's right might be) ?

It is a very striking fact that none of the judges ever referred in the leading case to 16 7 V 33, 7, 17, though the latter section (which figures in the heading of the report) seems to have been relied on in the Court below, and to have been cited in argument The effect of that case on s 7 (" The driver of every hackney carriage which shall ply for hire at any place . shall drive" &c) *must be that* "place" means public place, and, in s 17 (2), "Every driver who shall refuse to drive such a carriage &c to any place" &c, *must mean*, as in s 7, every driver plying for hire at a public place Without this limitation the driver in *Case v Storey* must clearly have been convicted under s 17

Therefore, if the principle of *Case v Storey* is good law—and it has never been doubted—the word "place" appearing in the definition of hackney carriage in the Acts of 1831, 1843, and 1853 means public place The word does not disappear till the Act of 1869 (32-3 V 115)

Since that Act (passed a few months after *Case v Storey*, and, as regards s 4, expressly in view of the decision therein, according to a dictum of Willes, J., in *Allen v. Tunbridge*, L. R., 6 C. P. at 484) the situation is clearly put by Cockburn, C. J., in *Clarke v. Stanford* (L. R., 6 Q. B. at p. 359), 1871.

"Carriages are admitted within the premises of the railway company at Harrow under a contract by which they engage to convey any passengers who come by railway, and, although it is not expressly found so in the case, yet it is clear that the appellant's carriages are exclusively for the use of passengers who come by the railway. I assume that the use of the carriage is confined to the purposes of the passengers coming by railway, still, that is a plying for hire. Where a person has a carriage ready for the conveyance of passengers in a place frequented by the public, he is plying for hire, although the place is private property. The public is entitled to travel by railway, and has a right to pass over the premises of the railway to get out, and if a man is standing on those premises with his carriage to take the public, he is plying for hire. The Legislature has omitted the words 'public place'[1] [in Section 4], and this appears to have been done intentionally and advisedly."

Thus, as before the Act of 1869 a railway cabman was not bound to be hired because the station was not a public place, and under that Act a cab to be plying need not necessarily be in a public place, but the cabman is not bound to be hired—for the power to compel is wholly derived from 1-2 W. IV. 22, and 16-17 V. 33—it follows that such a cabman is not, *by statute*, bound to drive anyone at all. Such liability as he is under depends entirely upon his contract with the company. In this sense must be understood the decision of the magistrate who stated (*Case v. Storey*, L. R., 4 Ex. 320) that "privileged cabmen at stations could not be said to be plying for hire under, and when there governed by, the rules laid down in the Hackney Carriage Acts, but were, whilst within the station, governed in their dealings

---

[1] A slight inaccuracy. This *expression* does not occur in the definition of hackney carriage in any previous Act.

with the public by the ordinary law of contract." For the effect of this proposition on Fares see pp. 24, 57, *post*.

This reasoning proceeds on the assumption that the Act of 1869 is not to be read or incorporated with the Acts of 1831 and 1853 If they could be so connected, the effect of the new definition in s 4 of the former would be that the penalties denounced in the latter against recusant drivers under certain conditions descend at once upon that class always and everywhere, for the words "standing in any street or place" (1-2 W IV 22, 35) and "at any place" (6-7 V. 86, 2) would be repealed On Virtual Repeal or Repeal by Implication see *Hardcastle on the Construction of Statute Law*, Second Edition, p 352

But, except convenience (and that only from the hirer's point of view), there is nothing in the Act of 1869 to suggest or require that it should supersede or modify Acts *in pari materia* except where its object is expressly to do so On the contrary, (i) Par 2 of S 4 is governed by the opening words of the section "In this Act", and (ii) S 15 enacts, "All the provisions of the Acts relating to hackney carriages in force at the time of the commencement of this Act shall, subject to any alteration made therein by this Act continue in force" Further, if it had been intended that this Act should be read with the others. nothing would have been easier or more usual than to say so in so many words

Moreover, if, as has been said above, this Act was passed in view of the decision in *Case v. Storey*, it is natural that it should enact clearly and simply what it was deemed right to amend therein Now, of course, the "mischief" of that decision, so to say, was that if a railway station was not a public place there was no penalty against an unlicensed cab plying there, and so the Revenue suffered, and against this abuse the Act did—so it has been several times held (*e.g Allen v Tunbridge, Clarke v. Stanford, Fornett v Clark*, 41 J P 359) —effectually provide Indeed, it is mainly a licensing Act, and there can be no doubt that it was never intended to touch (a) the Court's decision that a railway cabman was not bound to take a non-passenger, (b) their implication that he was bound to take a passenger Moreover, if the new definition is to be read into the older Acts (a) is swept away, but this, it is submitted, is not the law It is true that in the Act there are three references to compulsion on the driver (Section 9, Sub sections 2 and 3, and Restriction 2 on Section 9), but a recognition of the existing law is far from incorporation of the statutes in which that law is written, to say nothing of the right (possibly exercised here) of the Legislature to enact new law

It may be added that the effect of incorporation in this instance would be the extension of a penal clause, for railway cabmen as well as all others would be liable to the penalties of 1-2 W IV 22, 17 and 35, and of 16-7 V 33, 17, and this is not to be assumed without the strongest reason (Dyke *v* Elliott, L R, 4 P C 191).

If the view here taken is correct, it follows that if a railway company makes no contract with the cabmen it authorises to ply on its premises, they are not bound to take any would-be hirer, and are at liberty to make what terms they choose with him (see p. 22)

It will have been noticed that two of the learned judges based their decisions in *Case v Storey* (p 20), on the ground that the "place" must be one where both driver and hirer have a right to be In one sense, the driver there had such a right—though perhaps, in another (that of Channell, B) he had not—but at any rate the fact that the would-be hirer had none at all was fatal to his case. Now it certainly follows from these two judgments that a driver who had his cab where he had no right to be, and ought not to be, would not be bound to take a would-be hirer, but such a situation it is difficult to conceive Perhaps, however, the case of *Foulger v Steadman* (L R, 8 Q B 65) supplies an instance There a cab driver, who would now be called "unprivileged," drove a cab into Railway Place, connected with Fenchurch Street Station, belonging to the same owners, "and which is not a *cul-de-sac*, but presents the appearance of a public street, through which foot passengers and carriages are allowed by the railway company to pass" The company allowed part of this property to be occupied as cabstands, on payment of a weekly sum by the drivers The respondent was not such a driver, and refused to leave the stand when requested to do so by an official An alderman refused to convict (apparently on the ground that the Place was a public thoroughfare, and that the cabmen was not a wilful trespasser), but the Queen's Bench (Blackburn, Hannen, and Quain, JJ) unanimously held that he was a wilful trespasser under 3-4 V 97, 16 (a Railway Act)

It would seem, then, that an unprivileged driver plying at a privileged stand—and, generally, a trespasser anywhere—is not bound to take a fare But the question is obviously one of no importance, for there is little fear of a cabman violating a well-known legal maxim by setting up his *turpitudo* in this way

Among persons who have a legal right to be at a railway station are not to be reckoned those going to meet trains. Therefore they have no legal right to hire a railway cab.

The first of these propositions was expressly held by the House of Lords (Lord Halsbury, C, Lords Watson, Macnaghten, and Davey, Lord Morris dissenting) in *Perth General Station Committee v. Ross* ([1897], H L App Cas 479)

Any cause of complaint on the part of travellers as to facilities for obtaining cabs at railway stations may be redressed through the Railway Commissioners.

See the judgment of Lord Watson (*ubi supra* at p 488), and also *ex parte Painter* (2 C. B, N S 703), 1857 In the latter case "a railway company granted exclusive permission to a limited number of fly proprietors to ply for hire within their station The Court [of Common Pleas] refused to grant a writ of injunction against the company under The Railway and Canal Traffic Act, 1854 (17-8 V 31), at the instance of a fly proprietor who was excluded from participation in this advantage, although it was sworn by the complainant and by several other fly proprietors, who were likewise excluded, that occasional delay and inconvenience resulted to the public from the course pursued" "Before we put the powers of the Act in motion," said Cresswell, J, "we must be satisfied that there is some substantial injury or inconvenience to the public, and that the complaint is *bonâ fide* made on behalf of the public." "The complaint," said Williams, J, "must come from those who use the railway" This jurisdiction of the Courts was transferred to the Railway Commissioners by 36-7 V 48, 6. See also *Marriott v London and South Western Railway Co* (1 C B, N S 499), 1857, and *Hole v. Digby* (27 W R 884)

CABS TO RAILWAY STATIONS

But if a railway station is not a place *from* which the driver is always bound to drive, it is a place *to* which and *into* which, speaking generally, he is bound to drive The question was expressly tested in the great cab strike of 1896, and so decided

In other words "to any place" in ss 7 and 17 of 16-7 V 33 includes a private place to which the cabman can get access

(*Ex parte Kippins* [1897], 1 Q B 1) The driver refused to drive beyond the gates of Euston Station, though requested to do so by the hirer, and informed by a railway official that he might A magistrate convicted the driver, and the Divisional Court (Grantham and Wright, JJ) refused a *rule nisi* for a *mandamus* to him to state a case

INABILITY TO PAY THE FARE.

Has a cabman the right of refusing to take a person whom, rightly or wrongly, he supposes to be impecunious? He has not. It is possible, but not probable, that in an extreme case of notorious inability to pay the fare, a justice might hold that there was a "reasonable excuse" within Section 7 of the Act of 1853 (cited above, p 16). There is no substantial injustice in this state of things, because if the cabman judged correctly that the would-be hirer was unable to pay the fare, the latter would, in all probability, be equally unable to pay the preliminary expenses of summoning the former (as to which see p. 31).

INFECTIOUS DISEASES &c.

A cabman in the County of London *must refuse* to take on his cab a person suffering from a dangerous infectious disease, and he *may refuse* to receive the corpse of anyone who has died from such a disease. He is not bound to take corpses of any other kind, but he is not prohibited from doing so

"It shall not be lawful for any owner or driver of a public conveyance knowingly to convey, or for any other person knowingly to place, in any public conveyance, a person suffering from any dangerous infectious disease [defined in s 58], or for a person suffering from any such disease to enter any public conveyance, and, if he does so, he shall be liable to a fine not exceeding ten pounds, and if any person so suffering is conveyed in any public conveyance, the driver or owner thereof, as soon as it comes to his knowledge, shall give notice to the sanitary authority, and shall cause such conveyance to be disinfected, and if he fails so to do, he shall be liable to a fine not exceeding five pounds, and the owner or driver of such conveyance shall be entitled to recover in a summary manner from the person so conveyed by him, or from the person causing that person to be so conveyed by him, a sum sufficient to cover any loss and expenses incurred by him in connection with such disinfection It shall be the duty of the sanitary authority, when so requested by the owner or driver of such public conveyance, to provide for the disinfection of the same, and they may do so free of charge" (Public Health (London) Act, 1891, 54-5 V. 76, 70)

"If (a) a person hires or uses a public conveyance other than a hearse for conveying the body of a person who has died from any dangerous infectious disease, without previously notifying to the owner or driver of the conveyance that such person died from infectious disease, or (b) the owner or driver does not, immediately after the conveyance has to his knowledge been used for conveying such body, provide for the disinfection of the conveyance, he shall, on the information of the sanitary authority, be liable to a fine not exceeding five pounds, and if the offence continues to a further fine not exceeding forty shillings for every day during which the offence continues" (Ibid s 74)

This Act only applies to the County of London (ss 132 and 141) Outside that area—and much of the Metropolitan Police District is outside that area—The Public Health Act, 1875, applies, and by s 127 a driver not only *may*, but *must*, after certain payment, take "any person so suffering" But possibly the London Act might be held to include the whole of the Metropolitan Police District in its operation, for s 132 provides that the Act "shall extend to places elsewhere so far as is necessary for giving effect to any provisions thereof in their application to London"

FARE BEFOREHAND.

A cabman has no right to demand his fare before carrying the hirer.

See a case reported in some London newspapers of 25th January, 1898, where a driver was fined for this offence at the Highgate

Petty Sessions. However, in another case in 1888 (for which see Blue Book 1386 to 1395, or the *Standard* of 16th January, 1888), a Metropolitan Police Magistrate refused to decide the point. It is submitted that the conviction was right, as even a conditional refusal is not permitted by the Act of 1853. The magistrates must be taken to have held that there was no "reasonable" excuse.

Perhaps the suggestion may be hazarded (it is believed for the first time) that cabmen should be empowered by law to demand the minimum fare (at present one shilling) in advance. This would effectually prevent their being cheated at any rate of their whole fare. It is difficult to see any objection to giving this power to any cabman who chooses to use it. It is merely the correlative of the power which the law already gives to the hirer to require a driver to drive, for a stated sum, a distance in the latter's discretion. If he chooses to exceed the exact legal distance, he may not ask more than the said sum under a penalty (1-2 W. IV. 22, 44).

These considerations lead to that of

THE REMEDIES OF BOTH PARTIES.

By "remedy" is not meant only the recovery of money, but revenge in the sense of infliction of punishment or penalty on the offender.

A.—REMEDIES OF THE HIRER

1. FARES.

First, as to disputes about fares, it may be mentioned that from 1853 to 1896 it was provided that—

"In case of any dispute between the hirer and driver of any hackney carriage, the hirer may require the driver forthwith to drive to the nearest Metropolitan police court or justice room, where complaint may be made to the magistrate then sitting, who shall hear and determine the same, without requiring any summons to be issued for that purpose, and if such dispute arise at a time when the police court or justice room is not open, the hirer may require the driver to drive to the nearest police station or justice room, where the complaint shall be entered, and notice given to both parties that the matter in dispute shall be heard by the magistrate at his next sitting" (16-7 V 33, 18)

This obviously clumsy procedure, if it was ever used, had become obsolete and was abolished by 59-60 V 27, 2.

2. OVERCHARGE.

There is a faint doubt about the point, but most probably an overcharge can be recovered summarily from a cabman It certainly can be recovered in a County Court as "money had and received," and the cabman certainly can be punished for making the overcharge

The doubt arises in the following way 1-2 W IV 22, 43, runs—

"No agreement whatever made with the driver of any hackney carriage for the payment of more than his proper fare, as the same is allowed and limited by this Act, shall be binding on the person making the same, but any such person may, notwithstanding any such agreement, refuse, on discharging such hackney carriage, the payment of any sum beyond the proper fare as allowed and limited as aforesaid, and in case any person shall actually pay to the driver of any hackney carriage, whether in pursuance of any such agreement or not, any sum exceeding his said proper fare which shall have been demanded or required by such driver, the person paying the same shall be entitled, on complaint made against such driver before any justice of the peace, to recover back the sum paid beyond the proper fare, and, moreover, such driver shall forfeit, as a penalty for such exaction, the sum of forty shillings; and in default of the repayment by such driver of such excess of fare, or of payment of the said penalty, such justice shall forthwith commit such driver to prison, there to remain for any time not exceeding one calendar month, unless the said excess of fare and the said penalty shall be sooner paid"

Now, the fares "allowed and limited by this Act" were contained in Schedules B and C—which were repealed in 1869 by 32-3 V 14, 39 (Customs and Inland Revenue Act)—and contained a scale different from that now in force. Meanwhile a new scale had come into force in 1853 under 16-7 V 33, 4 and 10, Schedule A, and 16-7 V. 127, 13 to 17. But the provision for the recovery of excessive fares has never been re-enacted, and consequently it may be argued that it only applies to the scale so carefully defined by this section and now no longer existing, and therefore that the section is now inoperative. It cannot be contended that any fare now chargeable which happens to coincide with that which would have been "allowed" for the same journey under the Act of 1831 is covered by the section as not being repugnant to it.

It is also to be noted that similar words in s 47 "according to the rates and fares contained in the Schedule C to this Act annexed" were expressly repealed by 37-8 V 35 (Statute Law Revision Act). The inference that the words in question in s 43 were designedly left is almost irresistible.

But, on the other hand, it is possible to maintain that the section is still, *mutatis mutandis*, alive. By s 3 the Act of 1843 incorporates that of 1831, leaving fares untouched. Consequently the Act of 1831 operates over the wider limits, the present ones, introduced in 1843. The first Act of 1853 incorporated by s 21 the Act of 1843, and, therefore, that of 1831. Moreover, s 21 says, "And all the provisions of the said Acts [that of 1843 and another], except so far as is herein otherwise provided, shall extend to this Act, and to all things done in execution of this Act." Now even assuming that the first Act of 1853 does not incorporate that of 1831, undoubtedly among the provisions of that of 1843 was the extension of s 43 and of Schedules B and C (of the 1831 Statute) to the wider London created by that of 1843 (and the same as that of 1853)—and such enactment therefore expressly holds good, "except so far as is herein otherwise provided." What "is herein otherwise provided" is the new Scale of Fares contained in the Schedule A of the first Act of 1853. It follows then that to s 43 of the 1831 Act Schedule A of that of 1853 is attached, in substitution for the old Schedules B and C. There can be little doubt that the Legislature did not intend to repeal the prohibition against the overcharge at which s 43 is aimed, and none whatever that it did not intend to set up two concurrent cab tariffs. Yet this would be the effect if the first Act of 1853 did not get rid of Schedules B and C in the 1831 Act. They were not expressly repealed till 1869.

That Sir John Bridge, the chief Metropolitan Magistrate, and the Home Secretary's Committee did not think that s 43 was virtually repealed may be gathered from the fact that the latter, following the former, agreed in recommending its express repeal in order to legalise agreements for more than the normal legal fare (*Report*, p 8) To accomplish this Sub-section 1 of s 17 of 16-7 V 33 would also have to be amended If s 43 of the 1831 Act is not operative there is no other legal means of dealing summarily with overcharges

For the sake of completeness it may be here added that fares were subsequently dealt with by 16-7 V 127, 13 to 15, and 32 3 V 115, 9 (3) (see p 52)

The former of these, the second Act of 1853 (s 17), expressly abstains from interfering with any provisions of any former Act in force, and so with s 43 of the 1831 Act, as it was in force in 1853 (*i e* without the reference to the Schedules) As the Act of 1869 prohibited any lowering of the fares, if s 43 operated on the scale of 1853 it also operates on the existing scale

A hirer who is unwilling to pay what he considers the excess over the proper fare may withhold that amount, and thus leave the cabman to his remedy (for which see p. 46). Custom and common sense require in that case that he should give the driver his name and address, and under the Act of 1896 he refuses to do so at his peril, if it turn out that the fare demanded was lawful (see p 18).

However, if he has paid or even been asked for more than the legal fare, the hirer may procure the infliction of a penalty upon the driver (see pp. 36, 37)

To do this he must apply, either personally or through a legal representative, to the magistrate who has jurisdiction where the act complained of took place within seven days of the offence (6 V. 86, 38, amending 1-2 W IV. 22, 63) If a summons is granted, he has to pay two shillings for it. He must then attend on the day fixed for the hearing, with his witnesses, if any. If he succeeds, he may be awarded costs at the discretion of the magistrate, unless the cabdriver is sent to prison, in which case the magistrate would not make him pay costs. Except in rare cases, none but costs actually paid for the summons will be awarded. If the hirer fails he would almost certainly be compelled to pay costs (for which see pp. 45, 46).

Anyone may make the complaint against the driver, and by doing so becomes a "common informer," but he is not, as a rule, entitled to any part of the penalty, if there is one. Under the Act of 1831 and other statutes he could recover a moiety, but this policy encouraged "the corrupt practices of common informers" and now he cannot be sure of recovering even under the statute of 1831 (1-2 W. IV 22, 71; 6-7 V 86, 46; 2-3 V 71, 34).

Practically, as has just been stated, anyone may make the complaint, when necessary; but in the case of a driver on private premises—for example, a railway station or quay, the only important instances—it may be that action must be taken through the private owner i.e. the company; but in effect the result is the same, for "privileged" cabs are certainly bound by stipulation with the companies to abide by the rules of other cabs and by other rules, too. In short, it is easier for an aggrieved passenger to "hit" a railway cabman than any other.

PENALTIES

The following list aims at enumerating fully the offences of which cabdrivers, as such, may be guilty, and the penalties therefor.

I.—As a rule, the offences created by the respective sections of the various Acts are different, but occasionally different penalties are provided in different Acts either for the same offence or for offences so expressed as to be practically indistinguishable. In the latter case the magistrate would have a discretion as to which penalty he would inflict if the offender was summoned under the Hackney Carriage Act of 1831, or that of 1843, or the first of 1853.

For applying the reasoning of p 30 above by force of 6-7 V 86, 3, and 16-7 V. 33, 21, these three Acts are to be read together. The words of s. 3 of 6-7 V. 86, "So much as relates to hackney carriages" almost certainly include what relates to the drivers thereof, the point of the limitation being the *non-inclusion* in that Act of the remaining subjects enumerated in the title of the Act of 1831. But, if it should be held that s 3 only incorporates enactments relating to the carriages (to the exclusion of the drivers), then the two latter Acts would not be read with the earlier

It might be a difficult question how far, by virtue of s 17, the second Act of 1853 (16-7 V 127) is to be read with the earlier Hackney Carriage Acts, but as, even before the repeal of the greater part of it, that Act enacted no penalty on drivers, such an inquiry would not be revelant here.

Otherwise, the justice must deal with the offender according to the particular statute under which he is summoned.

II.—In default of payment of a penal fine and of costs, the statute which imposes it indicates how the amount is to be recovered (viz. by distress on and sale of the offender's goods) *or* what other punishment (always imprisonment) is to be inflicted on him instead. But since The Summary Jurisdiction Act, 1879 (42-3 V. 49), this is of little practical importance, and it has not been thought worth while to set out in the list below the alternative punishment in each instance. The section, however, which appoints it is (except

D

when it is the same section) appended to that which deals with the primary penalty.

The matter is now partly regulated by s. 5 of the Act last mentioned which enacts—

> The period of imprisonment imposed by a Court of Summary Jurisdiction under this Act, or under any other Act, whether past or future, in respect of the nonpayment of any sum of money adjudged to be paid by a conviction, or in respect of the default of a sufficient distress to satisfy any such sum, shall, notwithstanding any enactment to the contrary in any past Act, be such period as in the opinion of the Court will satisfy the justice of the case, but shall not exceed in any case the maximum fixed by the following scale that is to say—
>
> | Where the amount of the sum or sums of money adjudged to be paid by a conviction, as ascertained by the conviction | The said period shall not exceed |
> |---|---|
> | Does not exceed 10s. | Seven days. |
> | Exceeds 10s but does not exceed £1 | Fourteen days |
> | " £1 " " £5 | One month |
> | " £5 " " £20 | Two months |
> | " £20 | Three months |
>
> And such imprisonment shall be without hard labour, except where hard labour is authorised by the Act[1] on which the conviction is founded, in which case the imprisonment may, if the Court thinks the justice of the case requires it, be with hard labour, so that the term of hard labour awarded do not exceed the term authorised by the said Act

The same statute empowers a Court of Summary Jurisdiction to mitigate, generally, the punishment it is required to impose, "under this Act or under any other Act," even to the extent of substituting a fine for imprisonment in cases where the original Act gives it no option of so doing (s 4)

Moreover, under the Hackney Carriage Acts themselves all penalties may be mitigated by the

---

[1] For example, The Hackney Carriage Acts, 1831 and 1843 It is not authorised by the first Act of 1853 (as now amended)

justice, and may, if he so order, be paid in instalments (1-2 W. IV 22, 70, and 6-7 V. 86, 39, 45). and under The Probation of First Offenders Act, 1887 (50-1 V 25) a justice has ample power to treat cabmen and others with such leniency as he may think fit.

III.—In addition to any other punishment—

(A) A driver's licence may be endorsed with a note of the offence of which he has been convicted, and of the penalty inflicted therefor (6-7 V 86, 21)

(B) A driver's licence may be revoked or suspended—

(i) Whenever it could have been so treated under statute on 11th August, 1869 (the date of the passing of the Metropolitan Public Carriage Act, 32-3 V 115)

(ii) For any breach of the Secretary of State's Order

(iii) For any breach of the Act of 1869

(Cl 18, Order of Secretary of State of 18th August, 1897, under 32 3 V. 115, 8)

By 6-7 V 86, 25, the licence of any driver "convicted of any offence, whether under this Act or under any other Act," and also any other licence which he shall hold under the provisions of this Act, "may be revoked or suspended by the justice." This Act is, as we have seen, to be read with the first Act of 1853, and almost certainly with that of 1831. As these are the only statutes dealing with drivers' licences in force before 1869, and as, as stated above, any breach of the Act of 1869 may entail this particular penalty, it follows that for *any* offence under the Hackney Carriage Acts (as well as under the Order) such a licence may be revoked or suspended

Penalties.

The asterisk attached to a number means that the penalty indicated also falls on the proprietors for the same or corresponding offence or their share therein e g No. 11 for not providing a check string

OFFENCE	MAXIMUM PENALTY	STATUTE
1 Refusing to be hired when not engaged	40s	1-2 W IV 22, 35, 63 16 7 V 33, 17 (1)
2 Refusing to take the number of passengers permitted, or less	40s.	16 7 V 33, 9, 17 (1)
3 Refusing to drive to any place in London (see p 11) distant six miles or less	40s	16-7 V 33, 7, 17 (2)
4 Refusing to drive for an hour or less	40s	16-7 V 33, 7, 17 (2)
5 Demanding or taking[1] more than the legal fare[2]	40s	16 7 V. 33, 4, 17 (1).

[1] "Take" in s 17 must mean against the will of the passenger (*e.g* in giving change) It cannot possibly mean that the driver is prohibited from taking a voluntary gift in excess of the fare

[2] Both Sections 4 and 17 contemplate only "the proper fare as set forth in Schedule A to this Act annexed" That schedule has never been repealed, and authorises a scale of charges different from that now in force (*e.g* sixpence for one mile) Thus a question arises similar to that discussed above in reference to overcharge (see p 20) Since this Act of 1853 some extra charges have been recognised, and fares have been enhanced by statute and under the Secretary of State s Order In effect, therefore, something is added to the Schedule, and there can be little doubt that as it stands it has been superseded by more recent legislation If words limiting a section—and that a penal one—being still unrepealed may be disregarded (see p 30), *a fortiori* the section is still alive when for such words others may be substituted Moreover, part of the schedule has not been superseded, and is still in force (see p 52)

That the Secretary of State thought that this sub section was still operative is clear from the fact that while the Order of 10th March, 1871, contained a similar provision (27), subsequent Orders have omitted it If it were not in force now there would be no means, statutory or otherwise, of punishing the offence of demanding merely

PENALTIES. 37

OFFENCE.	MAXIMUM PENALTY.	STATUTE
Demanding and getting[1] more than legal fare.	40s. Excess to be repaid (in default justice must commit to prison)	1-2 W. IV 22, 43.
6. Demanding more than stated sum[2] for which hirer has required him to drive (even if driver has gone beyond distance paid for)	40s	1-2 W. IV 22, 44, 63
7.* Demanding or exacting more than agreed sum, even though less than legal fare	40s	1-2 W. IV 22, 45, 63
8.* Demanding "back fare" (i.e for return from place of discharge).	40s.	16-7 V 33, 4, 19.
9 Refusing to take a reasonable quantity of luggage	40s	16-7 V 33, 10, 17 (1), 19
Demanding more than proper charge for luggage	40s	16-7 V 33, 10, 19.
10 Refusing to wait when deposit paid, not waiting for time so paid for, not accounting for deposit	40s.	1-2 W IV 22, 47, 63
11.* Not having and using check string and wire	20s.	1-2 W IV 22, 48; 63.
12.* Permitting strangers to ride without consent of hirer	20s	1-2 W. IV 22, 50, 63

[1] Repeal of this section was recommended (*Report*, 8)

[2] Presumably this sum must not be less than the minimum allowed at the time

OFFENCE	MAXIMUM PENALTY.	STATUTE.
13 Allowing anyone, besides himself if unhired, and if hired anyone except hirer or "person employed"[1] by him to ride on the box	20s.	6-7 V. 86, 33; 39.
14* Obstructing in plying (see Nos 49 to 51), improperly standing, improperly feeding horses in street (see No 47), refusing to give way, "if he conveniently can, to any private coach or other carriage", depriving another driver of his fare "in a forcible or clandestine manner"; obstructing another driver in taking up or setting down	20s	1-2 W. IV. 22, 51, 63.
15 Plying elsewhere than at an appointed standing, loitering, wilfully obstructing	20s.	6-7 V 86, 33, 39.
16 Causing bodily harm by "wanton or furious driving or racing or other wilful misconduct, or by wilful neglect"	Two years' imprisonment, with or without hard labour	24 5 V 100, 35 [2]
17* Injuring or endangering persons or property through intoxication or furious driving, wilful misconduct, using abusive language, "other rude behaviour", assaulting or obstructing police	£5 If proprietor[3] licence may be revoked and need not be renewed.	1-2 W. IV 22, 56, 63.

---

[1] The prohibition is probably due to the practice of servants riding on the box See the citation in the Introduction from the *History of Taxation*

[2] This applies to all persons. [3] Drivers were not licensed in 1831

PENALTIES

OFFENCE	MAXIMUM PENALTY.	STATUTE
18 Practically the same as No 17 (the person or property must be in a street or highway, see No 50), being drunk during employment, using insulting gestures.	£3 Two months with or without hard labour Compensation for injury up to £10	6-7 V. 86, 28, 39.
19 Leaving carriage unattended in a public place (see Nos 48 and 51).	20s Horse and carriage may be seized by a constable and sold to pay expenses, costs, &c.	1-2 W IV 22, 55; 63.
20 Standing or plying opposite the General Post Office	£5	7 W IV. & 1 V. 86, 8, 13
21 * Driving without a licence	£5, £10*	6-7 V 86, 10, 39
22 * Plying for hire without a licence	40s	32-3 V 115, 8[1], 13
23 Improperly transferring or lending licence, permitting anyone else to use ticket or badge.	£5	6-7 V. 86, 10, 39.
24* Knowingly plying for hire with unlicensed cab	£5 a day.	32-3 V 115, 7, 13.
Removing, concealing, altering, &c, authorised or affixing unauthorised plate mark or number, or conniving thereat	40s	30-1 V 134, 17 (2); 32-3 V 115, 6, 7; Order, 12 (D), 15, 18.
25 Procuring licence by false pretences	£5	6-7 V 86, 14 (1), 39
26 Not wearing badge (ticket) when employed or appearing before a justice, refusing to produce it for inspection	40s	6-7 V 86, 17, 39.

[1] This section expressly purports not to repeal 6 7 V 86, 10 A clear distinction is, therefore, made between the offences here numbered 21 and 22.

COMPENSATION.

Note to No 18, *supra*, p 39

In this case the magistrate may order the proprietor to pay any sum up to ten pounds by way of compensation to any party aggrieved, in addition to costs, and he may order the driver to pay such sum in the first instance. But it must be carefully noted that whoever *accepts* compensation in this form *cannot get any other by process of law*, however large his claim. Magistrates in offering such an award should point this out to the party concerned.

Wright v London General Omnibus Co (2 Q B D 271).—In this case the police had summoned two omnibus drivers for "racing," through which a cab was damaged. It is not stated whether the driver was hurt personally. He was a witness at the police court, and distinctly told the magistrate that ten pounds would not sufficiently compensate him. In the end, however, the magistrate awarded him five pounds against each of the drivers, *and he took those sums*. He then sued the proprietors (the company) for damages, and obtained a verdict for £95 in a County Court. But, though he had not been the complainant against the omnibus drivers, and had always disclaimed that ten pounds would satisfy his demand, a Divisional Court set aside the verdict, mainly on the ground that he had taken the money awarded, and, therefore, consented to the magistrate's jurisdiction. "The party damaged," said Cockburn, C J, "cannot obtain compensation both against the master and against the servant." He also remarked, "It was no doubt intended that the provisions of the section should only be put in force where the damage done was slight," and this, too, was the opinion of Mellor, J. It seems, then, that if the plaintiff had not taken the ten pounds action could have been maintained.

When, then, the sum claimed as compensation for injuries due to offences under this section, is more than ten pounds, there must be an action in the County Court or the High Court.

As to a Proprietor's responsibility for the negligence of, and his remedy against, a Driver see pp. 66 *et seq.*, 86

B—REMEDIES OF THE DRIVER.
1. AGAINST HIRERS.

It is convenient to consider first what protection the law affords to a cabman improperly summoned, *i.e.* brought before a justice and not convicted.

"If the driver of any hackney carriage shall, in civil and explicit terms, declare to any person desirous to hire such hackney carriage that it is actually hired, and shall afterwards, notwithstanding such reply, be summoned to answer for his refusal to carry such person in his said hackney carriage, and shall upon the hearing of the complaint produce sufficient evidence to show that such hackney carriage was at the time actually and *bonâ fide* hired, and it shall not appear that he used uncivil language, or that he improperly conducted himself towards the party by whom he shall be so summoned, the justice before whom such complaint shall be heard shall order the person who shall have summoned such driver to make to him such compensation for his loss of time in attending to make his defence to such complaint as such justice shall deem reasonable, and in default of payment thereof to (*sic*) commit such person to prison for any time not exceeding one calendar month, unless the same shall be sooner paid" (1-2 W IV. 22, 36)

There is a similar provision in s. 57 for compensation in other cases of unsubstantiated complaints under this Act.

And again, "if any person refuse or omit to pay the driver" his fare or "deface or injure his cab" the justice may grant a summons (or even a warrant), and in the result "award reasonable satisfaction . . . for his fare or for his damages and costs, and also a reasonable compensation for his loss of time" in going to the Court. In default of the penalty, the offender may be sent to prison for one month with hard labour (s. 41, where "defender" must be a misprint for "offender")

These sections (36, 41, and 57) are the only ones which give compensation for loss of time &c to drivers as such Of these only s 57 purports to be limited in scope to this Act. But if, as we have seen (p 30), the three earliest Hackney Carriage Acts are to be read together, this is of little consequence. At any rate, ss. 36 and 41 are not so limited. However, the usual procedure is now under the Summary Jurisdiction Acts (see below), where compensation may be given under the more comprehensive name of "costs."

A cabdriver who takes out a summons against a "fare" for any criminal offence is in the same position as any other person (see p 31).

But if he takes out a summons for a civil matter, by far the most common instance of which is when he claims more for his fare than he has received, he is in a favoured position as to costs. In the first place, however, he has to pay, in addition to the cost of the summons (two shillings), one shilling to the police for service of it (under 53-4 V. 45, 3). If he wins at the hearing, it is usual, at Bow Street and many other (if not all) Metropolitan Police Courts, to award him, in addition to these costs, half a crown for his loss of time in taking out the summons and the same amount for the hearing—eight shillings in all; and the justice has a discretion (rarely exercised) to award him more costs. It often happens that the summoned "fare" pays the sum claimed into Court. Where the scale of costs just mentioned is allowed, the same costs must be paid when the money is paid into Court, otherwise it is not accepted, and the case must be heard.

The practice in the City may, perhaps, be gathered from an answer of an ex-Lord Mayor of London (Sir James Whitehead) to the Committee of Enquiry in 1894.—"We always make the delinquent not only pay the cabman his full fare, but the costs of the summons and payment for the number of days or the number of hours the cabman may have been obliged to take away from his duty" (*Blue Book*, 6910).

A fare is a "civil debt" (42-3 V. 49, 6, 35).

The only case on the subject (*Reg. v Kerswill* [1895], 1 Q. B 1) is not a London case, but that makes the adoption of the judgment of the Divisional Court in London cases easier, for the difficulty as to the construction of 10-1 V 89, 66, which arose in that case (see the judgment of Mathew, J) does not arise here. "The matter," said that learned judge, "relates to one of the common transactions of life, which are not ordinarily the subject of criminal proceedings" "It is clear," said Charles, J , "that the mere statement in an Act of Parliament that a sum is recoverable as a penalty does not turn the nonpayment of what is merely a debt into an offence."

His dictum, "as judges have pointed out, 'information,' and 'complaint' are words which connote each other," should be noted

Sir John Bridge the chief Metropolitan Magistrate, thus explained the effect of Sections 6 and 35 of The Summary Jurisdiction Act of 1879 on this section (41) to the Committee of Enquiry in 1874:—

"There can be no imprisonment until the process is gone through which is for the recovery of civil debt. That process, among other things, makes it necessary that the complainant, before he can send a man to prison for not paying his fare, shall be able to prove that the man has the means to pay the fare, and of course that is information which it is almost impossible for a cabman to get without laying out a quantity of money and spending valuable time for him, which makes the redress under the Act of 1879 absolutely useless to him." The operation of that Act on this section "absolutely," he went on, "took away the value of it to them Whether or not it is quite right to say that it did repeal this section to that extent is, I think, a matter of some doubt. . . . Still, no person has ever ventured to say that this Act was still in force now, and it may be, but he would require to be a very brave man who would put it in force instead of the Act of 1879, because he [the magistrate] would be liable to an action if he were wrong, but in my opinion there is very good ground for thinking this Act is still in force . I think it is quite clear that to be just to the cabman some such remedy as is contained in section 41 ought to be given to him, because he is without practical redress at present" (*Blue Book*, 1768-9)

The learned magistrate appears to doubt whether any justice could now use his powers under this section to commit to prison, but can it be doubted that he might use them to *award*, if not to enforce, compensation? There might be many cases in which the cabman could easily "prove means." In any case, compensation to a cabman for loss of time can be awarded as costs under the Act of 1879

Finally, in 1896 was passed the London Cab Act, popularly known as the "Bilking" Act In 1894 the Home Secretary appointed a Committee of Enquiry to consider the Cab Service of London. The Committee reported early in 1895, and this Act was ultimately the fruit of their labours The "bilker" they defined as "the man who, by disappearing altogether, evades payment of his fare" (*Report*, p 5).

The important part of the Act is set out above (p 18) The main difficulty still remains of catching the "bilker" But, except in the case of honest dispute as to fare, the Act has got over the difficulty suggested by Sir John Bridge by substituting for process for "civil debt" that for an "offence," and so making the offender liable for compensation.

A driver can, of course, sue for his fare in a County Court, but this is probably his least convenient remedy, except where he has given credit and the time for summary process has expired.

As to the remedy of a driver against a person who causes him to take a passenger suffering from a dangerous infectious disease see p. 27.

A driver who takes property left in his cab to the nearest police station is entitled to receive from the successful claimant any expenses incurred, and also "such reasonable sum" as the Commissioner of Police may award. Such property not successfully claimed within one year from its deposit is to be sold or otherwise disposed of, and out of the proceeds all expenses incurred and a "reasonable sum" for the driver are first to be paid (16-7 V. 33, 11)

By 32-3 V. 115, 9 (5), the Home Secretary is empowered to make regulations "fixing the charges to be paid in respect thereof, with power to cause such property to be sold or to be given to the finder in the event of its not being claimed within a certain time"

Accordingly, the last Order of the Secretary of State (dated 18th August, 1897, and having force from 1st September, 1897) contained a clause (30) providing that if any such property "be not within three months claimed, and proved to the satisfaction of the Commissioner to belong to the claimant, the Commissioner shall forthwith sell such property, and out of the proceeds shall award to such driver . . . " as follows:—

For Property consisting of or comprising any gold or silver money, bank notes, jewellery, or watch, and being of less value than £10	A sum equal to 3s in the £ on the value of the property
For Property of any other kind, and being of less value than £10	A sum equal to 2s 6d in the £ on the value of the property
For Property of the value of £10 or upwards	Such sum as the Commissioner shall deem reasonable

But "the Commissioner may, if he think fit, at the expiration of the said period of three months, deliver the property to such driver .... instead of awarding to him a sum of money." The same scale obtains when there is a successful claimant (Clause 31)

It will be noticed that there is a very serious discrepancy between the time—a year—mentioned in the Act of 1853, and that prescribed in the Secretary of State's Order (Clause 30). viz. three months. It is suggested, with submission, that it is doubtful whether this term of the Order can prevail against the Statute

Section 15 of the Act of 1869 says —

"All the provisions of the Acts relating to hackney carriages in force at the time of the commencement of this Act shall, subject to any alteration made therein by any order or regulation of the Secretary of State made in pursuance of this Act, continue in force" &c

Is, then, this regulation made *in pursuance of this Act*? Section 9 (5) empowers the minister to make regulations "for securing the safe custody and redelivery of any property accidentally left in hackney carriages, and fixing the charges to be paid in respect thereof, with power to cause such property to be sold, or to be given to the finder, in the event of its not being claimed within a certain time"

It is submitted that that "certain time" must be deemed to be that which was at the date of this enactment fixed by statute, and that here no power is given to *override* the section (11) in question. It is certainly not given expressly, than which nothing was easier if the Legislature intended to give it, and the proposition that the "certain time" is to be fixed by the Secretary of State certainly cannot be inferred from the words. The case is wholly different with respect to the power to fix fares &c under Section 9 (3), for there the power is expressly given, and the sub-section is a nullity without it (see p 52).

An instance is given below (see p. 60) of a previous Order conflicting with a statute, and invalid to that extent.

It should be noticed that regulations for fixing rates and fares or other matters may be superseded by the corporation of any borough within the Metropolitan Police District by virtue of statutory power, but such regulations must be first approved by a Secretary of State Thus The Croydon Corporation Act, 1884 (47-8 V. 41, 53), conferred such powers—of course, only within the borough. It is conceivable that this concurrent jurisdiction might lead to considerable inconvenience, but, so far, the matter is of small practical importance.

2. Against Proprietors.

As to the remedies of Drivers against Proprietors see pp. 86, 87, 89.

FARES.

Fares and charges are fixed chiefly by the Secretary of State's Order, and to a small extent by statute.

The Secretary of State derives his authority from 32-3 V 115, 9 (3), which says he "may from time to time, by order, make regulations for all or any of the following purposes that is to say—

For fixing the rates or fares, as well for time as distance, to be paid for hackney carriages and for securing the due publication of such fares provided that it shall not be made compulsory on the driver of any hackney carriage to take passengers at a less fare than the fare payable at the time of the passing of this Act."

When the Act of 1869 was passed the following statutes regulated fares —

(A) 16 7 V 33, Schedule A (1853)
(B) 16-7 V 127, 13, 14, 15 (1853)
(C) 30-1 V 134, 26 (1867)

None of these enactments has been repealed

For the sake of historical completeness it may be added that Schedules B and C of 1 2 W IV 22, which contained a Scale of Fares, were repealed in 1869 (32 3 V. 14, 39)

As to (A), in every respect in which the Secretary of State has made a change it has been in favour of the cabman In those particulars, therefore, this Schedule is superseded In two points he has not touched it, and the Schedule is therefore still operative —

1 For Two-horse Cabs the fare for a mile or less is 8d, or 2s. 8d. for an hour or less. If this were of any practical moment at the present day, it would doubtless need to be altered.[1]

2 No driver is bound to be hired by time between 8 p m and 6 a.m

(B) Section 13 introduced the differential fares beyond the radius But the enhanced rate (a shilling a mile) only began at the end of the radius, and only then if the cab was discharged beyond it.

(C) introduced the minimum fare of one shilling

---

[1] It is recorded, however, that after a heavy fall of snow two horse cabs plied in London on 2nd January, 1867 The same thing happened after the great snowstorm of January, 1881 (*The Times*, 19th and 20th January, 1881)

All other statutory fares are incorporated in the Order.

The Secretary of State may, if he choose, fix more than one scale of fares. *i.e* for different, or different classes of, vehicles (*Bocking v Jones*, L R, 6 C P 29, in 1870, Brett, J, doubting) "It might possibly," said Willes, J, "have been more convenient to divide the licensed hackney carriages into classes, and to have allowed a fixed rate, say of 1s 6d, 1s, and 6d per mile respectively," clearly implying that the Secretary has the power under the Act of 1869 See also the judgment of Bovill, C J

As to the suggestion of different classes of cabs, Sir Godfrey Lushington, Permanent Under-Secretary of State for the Home Department, told the Committee of Enquiry in 1894 —"It was attempted in 1869 and it ignominiously failed" (*Blue Book*, 9330)

Hiring is either (1) by distance, or (2) by time, at the option of the hirer. If he says nothing, it is by distance.

16-7 V 33, Schedule A, Order, 21

1. *By Distance*

The Statue of Charles I at Charing Cross is fixed upon as the centre of a circle with a radius of four miles This point was first chosen in 1853 (16-7 V. 127, 13). Originally, it is interesting to notice, the radius of the cab circle was three miles long and its centre at the General Post Office[1] (1-2 W IV. 22, 40) The *circumference* formed "the limits of the Metropolis."[2]

---

[1] Since 1829 at St Martin's le Grand, previously in Lombard Street

[2] This must not be confused with "the limits of the Act," which meant a circle with the same centre but a radius of five miles In 1838 "the limits of the Act" were extended to ten miles (1-2 V 79, 1), but this Act was totally repealed in 1843 (6 7 V 86, 1)

It may be noticed that the Act of 1843 contains the expression "the limits of this Act" (s 36), though it is nowhere defined in the Act However, the definition of "hackney carriage" in s 2 makes it quite clear that the present limits are intended Moreover, this Act is to be read with 16 7 V 33 by s 21 of the latter, and in s 20 "the limits of the Act" are defined (see also 16-7 V. 127, 17).

Distance is not measured as the crow flies, but along the shortest practicable route (*Blue Book*, 1063-4).

But now it is provided by The Interpretation Act, 1889 —

"In the measurement of any distance for the purposes of any Act passed after the commencement of this Act, the distance shall, unless the contrary intention appears, be measured in a straight line on a horizontal plane" (52-3 V 63, 34)

There is a case reported in the *Times* of 5th October, 1853, in which a magistrate held that if a road was "up," the fare for the "next nearest route" was due

In case of dispute as to the actual distance traversed, a magistrate may order the question to be settled by the test of the official measuring wheel (pedometer), which is kept at police courts, at a cost of seven shillings and sixpence, to be paid by the losing disputant But this test cannot be employed unless the case is before the magistrate for adjudication.

Books or Tables of Distances published by the authority of the Commissioner of Police are conclusive evidence of the distance therein enumerated (see 32 3 V 115, 9 (4) , 16 7 V 33, 6)

SCALE OF FARES (ORDER, 22-24).

1. When the whole journey is within the four-mile circle —

	s	d.
For two miles or less	1	0
For more than two miles (any part of a mile to count as a mile) per mile	0	6

2 When the journey is begun outside the four-mile circle, wherever ended.—

	s	d
For each mile and for any part of a mile	1	0

3. When the journey is begun within the four-mile circle and ended outside:—

> Up to the circumference the ordinary scale (as in 1) obtains, and outside the circle the ordinary scale (as in 2) obtains.

The fare for any mile begun within the circle but ended without is 1s.

Thus the fare for a journey from Charing Cross to a point 5½ miles distant would be 4s. (viz. 2s to the circumference or "radius mark," 1s for the whole mile and 1s. for the half-mile beyond it). Again, the fare for a journey from a point within the circle two and three-quarter miles distant from the circumference to a point a mile and a third beyond would be 4s. The total distance is four and one-twelfth miles; the first two miles cost 1s., the next mile being partly within and partly without the circle costs 1s., and the remainder, a mile and a twelfth, counts as two miles, and, being wholly without the circle, costs 2s.

Thus, too, the fare for a shorter distance may be greater than that for a longer. From a point half a mile inside the circle to one a mile without, 2s. From a point one mile inside the circle to one a mile without, 1s 6d.

The anomaly has often been noticed whereby there is a considerable difference in the fare for the *same* distance according as the journey is begun inside the circle and finished outside, or *vice versâ*. Thus, the fare from a point a mile outside the circle to Charing Cross would be 5s. (Scale 2 above), while the same journey in the reverse direction would cost 3s. (Scale 3). Partly to correct this state of things, the Home Secretary's Committee recommended, in concurrence with the London County Council, "that the radius should be that of the Administrative County of London, but minus the Plumstead district" (*Report*, p. 9).

2. *By Time.*

1. When the whole journey is within the four-mile circle :—

	Four wheeler.		Hansom.	
	s.	d.	s.	d.
For one hour or less	2	0	2	6
For a quarter of an hour, or any part of one, after one hour	0	6	0	8

N.B.—Here and in the charge for waiting (p 59) are the only differences in the fares of hansoms and four-wheelers.

2. When the journey is begun outside the four-mile circle, wherever ended :—

	s.	d.
For an hour or less	2	6
For a quarter of an hour, or any part of one, after one hour	0	8

3. When the journey is begun within the four-mile circle, and ended outside :—

As in 2

A driver may, if he choose, take less than the legal fare. This would be a special contract.

LIMITATIONS OF HIRING

No driver is bound to drive more than six miles (16-7 V. 33, 7; Order, Clause 27; 32-3 V. 115, 9, Restriction 2). No driver is bound to drive by time for more than one hour (16-7 V. 33, 7; Order, Clause 27), nor at all between 8 p.m and 6 a.m. (16-7 V. 33, Schedule A.).

No driver is bound to go beyond the Metropolitan Police District.

FARES IN CASES WHERE DRIVER IS NOT LEGALLY BOUND TO BE HIRED.

E.g. the cases suggested in the last paragraph. In the absence of express stipulation the legal fares would hold good even if the journey terminated outside the Metropolitan Police District. In all such cases it is obviously best to make a special contract beforehand.

Cabs hired at railway stations are subject to the ordinary fares.

"Section 42 [of 1-2 W IV 22]," said Bramwell, B, "imposes on the driver of a numbered cab a penalty for asking more than the statutory fare in unqualified terms, and without regard to the place where and the person by whom he was hired in the first instance It might perhaps be said that section only applies when a driver is *bound* to agree to be hired upon anybody's request, and not where he has an option, as at a railway station, but I think it applies to all drivers when once hired, no matter where" (*Case v Storey*, L R, 4 Ex 325) Section 42 has been repealed, but it is submitted that the principle here laid down holds good

It may safely be assumed that one of the conditions on which railway companies admit cabs into their stations to ply for hire is that the legal tariff is adopted. See, for instance, the Regulations of the Great Northern Railway Co. (*Blue Book,* pp. 316 and 317)

SUNDAY.

Drivers are expressly empowered to ply on Sundays, and their legal rights and duties are exactly the same as on any weekday (1-2 W. IV 22, 37) Formerly the licences were either for six days or for seven (16-7 V. 127, 11, and 29-30 V. 64, 10, both repealed by 32-3 V 14)

CABMEN AS MESSENGERS OR CARRIERS.

Clearly drivers are not bound to take messages or transport luggage without a passenger, as they are licensed primarily for the purpose of carrying passengers, and it would obviously be against public policy that they should be entitled to refuse a fare because they were employed on such errands. There is no legal tariff for such jobs There are no cases on the subject (but see p 67).

OTHER OR EXTRA PAYMENTS.

1. *Waiting at request of Hirer.*

This charge can obviously only apply to a distance-hiring. For waiting a full quarter of an hour, not necessarily at a stretch, but in stoppages making altogether fifteen minutes, the rate is for a four-wheeler hired within the four-mile circle, 6d., for all other cabs it is 8d. There is no charge for waiting less than a quarter of an hour in all, but there is the same charge for each quarter of an hour's delay (Order, 26).

2 *More than Two Passengers.*

The driver has the right, when required to wait, to "a reasonable sum as a deposit over and above the fare" he has already earned, but it seems that this right is little used. He must account for any sum so received when he is finally discharged (1-2 W. IV. 24, 47; see Penalty No. 10, p. 37)

For every person above two, there is an extra payment of 6d., irrespective of distance or length of time (16-7 V. 127, 14; Order 25 (2)). By Schedule A of 16-7 V 33 there was only 6d. extra for *any* excess over two persons (*per* Cockburn, C J, *Norton v Jones*, 8 L T., N. S 241).

But there is an exception in favour of

CHILDREN.

Two children under ten count as one person for the extra payment (over that for two passengers), and so does one child. But that is in respect of the extra payment *only*. Two children do not count as one person until there is an excess over two passengers. Thus, four children under age (being the only passengers) would not count as two persons but as three; there is no question of extra payment until two persons have been paid for, and so in the instance supposed there would be one extra payment of 6d.

<small>It is, however, conceivable that four children equal two adult persons for payment generally. But in the Statutes and the Order the exception is only introduced in connection with excess over two passengers, or with the legal complement the cab may take (*Ibid.*, and Order, 20).

Notwithstanding the decision in *Norton v. Jones* (8 L. T., N. S. 241; 11 W. R. 373), where in 1863 the Queen's Bench (Cockburn, C. J., Crompton, Blackburn, and Mellor, JJ.) laid it down unanimously that one child under ten must be paid for as an extra person (*i.e.* 6d.), the Secretary of State's Order of 1871 fixed the extra payment in such a case at 3d. (Clause 24 (2)). This was clearly invalid, and has been omitted in subsequent orders. The Act of 1869 expressly prohibited any lowering of the fares then legal (32-3 V. 115, 9 (3)).</small>

In respect of the legal complement of passengers, two children under ten count as one person. A four-wheeler, therefore, might take ten such children (Order, 20).

SPEED.

A driver hired by distance is bound to go at the rate of six miles an hour unless requested to go slower: if hired by time, at that of four.

This is the only interpretation which avoids a clear contradiction between Sections 7 and 17 of the Act of 1853. Section 7 says:—

"Provided always that when any hackney carriage shall have been hired by time, the driver may be required to drive at any rate not exceeding four miles within one hour," and if he be required to go faster, there is a higher fare after four miles (viz in addition to that by time that by distance)

If this provision were used nowadays, the scale now in force would have to be substituted for that of Schedule A of this Act (see p. 52).

Section 17 says:—

"Every driver . . . who shall not drive the same [i.e his cab] at a reasonable and proper speed, not less than six miles an hour, except in cases of unavoidable delay, or when required by the hirer thereof to drive at any slower pace," incurs a penalty

---

LUGGAGE.

A driver may not refuse to carry a reasonable quantity of luggage for the hirer (16-7 V 33, 10, 17 (1)) "If any luggage is carried outside the hackney carriage he shall be entitled to an extra payment of twopence for every package carried outside, whatever may be the number of persons carried" (Order, 25 (1))

The Order is more favourable to the driver than the regulation of Schedule A of the Act of 1853, which previously controlled this rate

In this instance the Secretary of State was empowered to alter the statute. 32-3 V 115, 15, enacts —

"All the provisions of the Acts relating to hackney carriages in force at the time of the commencement of this Act [11th August, 1869] shall, subject to any alteration made therein by this Act, or by any order or regulation of the said Secretary of State made in pursuance of this Act, continue in force"

Section 9 (3) of the same Act empowers him to make regulations "for fixing the rates or fares, as well for time as distance, to be paid for hackney carriages," thus clearly giving him authority to alter the tariff in force

It is true that nothing is expressly said about luggage, but as the subject was previously dealt with in Schedule A (16-7 V 33), which was headed "Rates and Fares to be paid for any Hackney Carriage &c," it is only reasonable to suppose that the Legislature, in adopting that phraseology, intended to convey jurisdiction over the whole contents to which it referred. Nevertheless, it is desirable that the matter should be put on a clear legal basis. At a convenient opportunity 16 7 V. 33, 10, and Schedule A. might with advantage be repealed

What is "Luggage"? With reference to cabs there is, apparently, no reported definition of a Superior Court

On 13th May, 1853, the *Times* mentions a case in which a driver was blamed by the magistrate for carrying 130 pineapples inside as luggage, and was fined forty shillings for seeking to charge for them as such

"Luggage," says Archibald (*Metropolitan Police Guide*, Second Edition, 1065), "would seem to mean personal luggage. Magistrates are reported to have held that it does not include such things as a case of pineapples, a sheep's carcase in a canvas sheet, &c., and that, if carried in a hansom, it must be considered as outside if not entirely within the doors when closed, or behind a perpendicular line from the front part of the top of a hansom."

In these circumstances we must take a hint from the law as to luggage on railways. Where a statute spoke of "ordinary luggage," Lush, J. (with whom the rest of the Court of Queen's Bench, viz. Hannen and Hayes, JJ., concurred), said:—

"It must have been intended that the passenger should be allowed to carry something more than that which he requires for his own personal use and convenience. The only definition I can think of, and one which is sufficient for this case, is that the words of the statute describe a class of articles which are ordinarily or usually exercised by travellers as their luggage. I think we must confine the definition of personal luggage in the sense that I have mentioned, namely, to that description of goods which passengers usually carry as part of their luggage" (*Hudston v Midland Railway Co*, L R, 4 Q B 370-1)

Each case then must be decided on its circumstances, regard being had to the normal habits of cab riders and to the fundamental difference in the accommodation which trains and hackney carriages respectively can physically afford. *Solvitur currendo*.

For the Police Memorandum to Drivers on this subject see Appendix B.

Clearly a cabman is not bound to take animals.

Bicycles are not "luggage" on cabs.

See an action against a proprietor reported in *The Times* of 9th October, 1897. There the Judge of the Lambeth County Court expressly held this proposition, "and suggested that, in view of the fact that cycles could not be legally defined as luggage, cyclists should, before entrusting their machines to cabmen, have a clear understanding that they were being conveyed on the same conditions as luggage." It was stated in argument that "one of the London stipendiary magistrates recently held that bicycles were not luggage."

[It is not clear from the report whether the driver was guilty of negligence; that point, however, would not affect the decision here considered. See the case commented in *Law Journal*, 1897, p 502.]

LIGHTING.

In 1867, power was given to the Commissioner of Police to prescribe a time between sunset and sunrise during which a cab must have "at least one lamp properly trimmed and lighted" (30-1 V 134, 17 (1)). Masters and men objected so strongly to the Commissioner's Order (on the ground of expense) that the latter struck on 3rd December, 1867; other grievances were alleged, but this was said to be the "last straw." Legislation to relieve them in this respect was immediately promised, and the strike ended. A few days later it was enacted that no regulation under the obnoxious section should be made except with the approval of a Secretary of State (31-2 V 5, 2). Mindful, probably, of the protest in 1867, the Home Secretaries from that year till 1875 did not give such approval, and in 1875 both the sections just cited were repealed (by 38-9 V 66).

The Act of 1869, after giving (s. 9) the Secretary of State power to make certain regulations, goes on—

"Subject to the following restrictions (3) During such portion of time between sunset and sunrise as is from time to time prescribed, no driver shall ply for hire unless the hackney carriage under his charge be provided with a lamp properly trimmed and lighted, and fixed outside the carriage in such manner as is prescribed"

"Prescribed" here, by s 4, means "prescribed by Order" of a Secretary of State

It may be that these words in the Act of 1869 confer *by implication* a power on the Home Secretary to make regulations as to lighting, but such a power is nowhere expressly given

On the contrary, these words expressly purport to be a *restriction* on his power. If it were intended to give him power for this purpose the natural place to do so was immediately before these "restrictions" in the list of purposes enumerated in s 9, for which power is given *for the first time* to the Secretary of State to make regulations Moreover, at the time of the passing of this Act, the power to make a regulation on this subject was vested in the Commissioner of Police. The other two "restrictions," it may be noticed, save existing rights viz (1) those of the Lord Mayor, (2) those of the drivers, and (3) *may* have been intended to do the same for the Commissioner of Police

In any case, the want of time and conditions prescribed reduces these words in (3) to a nullity, for no Home Secretary has ever made any such regulation.

Consequently there is now no statutory regulation on the subject.

However, very recently (October, 1898) the London County Council has, by virtue of 51-2 V 41, 16, made the following Bye-law for the Administrative County of London —

"Every carriage, cart, waggon, or other vehicle which shall be driven or be upon any highway during the period between one hour after sunset and one hour before sunrise, shall be provided with a lamp or lamps, which shall be so constructed and placed (such lamp or one of such lamps being on the right or off-side of the carriage, cart, waggon, or other vehicle) as to exhibit a white light in the direction in which the vehicle proceeds, and shall be so lighted and kept lighted as to afford adequate means of signalling the approach or position of the vehicle This Bye-law shall not apply to any carriage which is required to carry lights by any statutory enactment, or by any rule, regulation, or order made under any statutory enactment, and for the time being in force"

A similar regulation has been made for the Administrative Counties of Middlesex, Surrey, and Kent, and for the Boroughs of Kingston-on-Thames and Richmond. The maximum penalty for non-compliance is 40s

Do these regulations apply to cabs in the City and in those parts of the Metropolitan Police District which are within the areas just enumerated? The point is doubtful, but probably they do. As we have seen, the authorities did not use their powers when they had them, and consequently, till these Bye-laws, there was from 1867 no compulsion in this matter on drivers The last sentence of the London County Council's Bye-law seems to be framed in view of the contingency of the Home Secretary making regulations, but there is nothing to prevent any other authority using any legal power it may possess. In the circumstances, it would not be safe for any cabman to violate the regulations. It will be noticed that they do not extend to all parts of the Metropolitan Police District.

As to Motor Cabs see the Order of the Local Government Board (Art. II. (9), Appendix D).

LOST LUGGAGE, INJURY, DAMAGE, &c.

The proprietor of a cab is liable for any loss or damage arising from the driver's negligence, if the hirer has himself taken all due care.

In *Ross v. Hill* (2 C. B. 877), 1846, it was admitted that the cabdriver was the servant of the proprietor, and the latter's liability for lost luggage was affirmed.

There Tindal, C.J., in his judgment clearly implies that the cab proprietor is not a common carrier. In *Brind v. Dale* (2 M. & R. 80, 8 C. & P. 207), 1837, the liability of a "town carman"[1] for lost luggage was discussed, and Lord Abinger, C.B., expressed a strong opinion that he was not a common carrier and, although the cart of a "town carman" is not a hackney carriage, it seems clear that a cab proprietor is not a common carrier on much the same grounds.

"Still," said Lord Abinger, "there are cases in which, although a person is not a common carrier, he is liable for the neglect of his own servants. I take it that if a man agrees to carry goods for hire, although not a common carrier, he thereby agrees to make good losses arising from the negligence of his own servants, although he would not be liable for losses by thieves or by any taking by force, or if the owner accompanies the goods to take care of them, and was himself guilty of negligence &c."

---

[1] A person who conveyed goods, not between fixed points or at fixed rates, but undertaking jobs as he could get them, and making a bargain in each case.

The last sentence clearly covers the case of luggage taken inside with the passenger, who must look after it himself with all reasonable diligence.

It is only for a passenger's luggage (or that of his party) that the proprietor can, in case of negligence, become liable. In other words, there cannot be a double hiring.

In a recent (1898) Scotch case the facts were as follows —

A engaged a cab to take him to a railway station, on the way the driver agreed with B to take a portmanteau thither for him at the same time without obtaining A's consent, though A, when he saw the portmanteau, did not order it to be taken down. On the way it was lost through the driver's negligence—*i e* when it fell off, probably through having been put on hurriedly and not properly secured A. refused to let the driver stop to pick it up

It was held unanimously by the Court of Session that the cab-owner was not responsible for the loss of the portmanteau, as the driver, after his cab had been hired by A, had no power to bind his master in a second contract of hiring with the owner of the portmanteau "The idea of such a joint hire of the cab as is suggested here is extravagant" (*per* Lord Young) "It was beyond the scope of the driver's employment to enter into such an anomalous contract" (*per* Lord Moncrieff) —*Ord v Gemmell & Son, Limited*, Sessions Cases, 5th Series, Vol. I, Part I, p. 17

As the cab proprietor is not a common carrier, he is subject to the ordinary law of negligence.

In *Powles v Hider* (6 E & B 207), 1856, the principle of *Ross v Hill*, though that case was not mentioned, was distinctly re-affirmed. The ordinary relations between driver and proprietor existed *i e.* the former, through whose negligence the plaintiff's trunk was lost, hired the horse and cab from the latter for so many hours at a fixed price Lord Campbell, C J, in holding (with the concurrence of Erle and Crompton, JJ) that the plaintiff could recover, said —

"Looking to the position of the proprietor and driver of a cab under the circumstances proved, and to the Acts of Parliament which regulate their respective duties, we are of opinion that the driver is to be considered the servant or agent of the proprietor, with authority to enter into contracts for the employment of the cab on which the proprietor is liable There can be no doubt that this would be so if the driver were engaged at fixed wages, accounting to the proprietor for all the earnings of the cab. But must not the actual arrangement between them be equally considered a mode by which the proprietor receives what may be estimated as the average earnings of the cab, *minus* a reasonable compensation to the driver for his labour? [An echo of *Morley v Dunscombe*, 11 L T 199, in 1848, cited and followed here.] This is quite different from hiring a job carriage or a carriage and horses to be driven by the hirer or his servant, where the hirer becomes bailee, and can in no sense be considered the servant of the proprietor. The Acts of Parliament referred to always regard the proprietor and driver of the hackney cab as employer and employed, or master and servant, and clearly contemplate that the party who engages the cab under the care of the driver shall have a remedy against the proprietor."

In *Milson v Silvester* (reported in *The Times* of 23rd April, 1863), the plaintiff had met with an injury owing to a cabdriver, who was in charge of a horse and cab belonging to the defendant, leaving his horse unattended. The judge (Wightman, J) elicited from the defendant that if he met the driver in the course of the day and did not approve of his mode of driving, he could dismiss him at the moment and get on the box himself. "The question then became one of damages only" i e the relation of master and servant clearly existed. The criterion is the extent of the master's control (see p 72).

Fowler v Lock (L R, 7 C P 281; 9 C P 751, 10 C P 90), 1872, is a peculiarly interesting case of injury, because the plaintiff was himself the driver of the defendant's cab. It is the first case in which *Powles v Hider* was considered. The plaintiff took his cab on the usual terms. "The horse with which the driver was furnished, which was fresh from the country and had never before been harnessed to a cab, bolted and overturned the cab, and injured the driver." The jury at the trial, under the direction of the judge, found that the defendant, when he let the horse, did not know that it was vicious and unfit for a cab &c, and this verdict was not seriously questioned. They also found that the horse was not reasonably fit to be driven in a cab, and that the accident was attributable to the horse, and they gave the plaintiff £50 damages. Two questions were reserved for the Court of Common Pleas

1. Was the plaintiff the servant of the defendant in such sense that, within the decided cases on the subject, he, the plaintiff, could not recover in respect of injuries sustained in the ordinary course of his employment?
2. Supposing the relation of master and servant in that sense did not exist, but that the relation was analogous to that of bailor and bailee, was there an implied contract by the former that the thing hired was reasonably fit for the purpose for which it was hired?

Grove, J, and Byles, J (who had tried the case below and was satisfied with the verdict), decided both these questions in favour of the plaintiff, holding "that the relation between the parties was that of bailor and bailee, and consequently that upon the finding of the jury the proprietor was responsible for the injury sustained by the driver"

"I feel obliged," said the former (p 280), "to come to the conclusion that the cabman is not the servant of the cab owner in the sense . of rendering the latter exempt from liability to the former in cases where a party not bearing the relation of master to servant would be liable"

"The driver," said Byles, J, "as between the cab owner and himself seems to me to have the complete and exclusive control and disposition of the vehicle within a certain district and not to be a servant of the proprietor, and therefore, by the terms of the contract, entitled to be furnished with a suitable, at least with a quiet or manageable, horse. . . Moreover, it has been held, and very recently, in this Court, in *Warren v Wildee* (Law Rep. W N, 1872, p 87), that a master is liable to his servant if he expose the servant to unreasonable risk and the servant be thereby injured, and that this is a question which ought to be left to the jury" Obviously, this reasoning applies, *mutatis mutandis*, to the cab as well as to the horse

Willes, J, however, dissented, holding that the relation was, as usual, that of master and servant (or at most co adventurers), and therefore, that in the absence of evidence of personal negligence or misconduct on his part, the owner was not responsible "It," said the learned judge, "the cab owner had been guilty of knowingly sending out an unfit horse with a driver who was not aware of the fact, there would have been a case of liability The remaining alleged ground of liability is therefore within the ordinary risk of the employment which the plaintiff undertook"

The case was taken on appeal to the Court of Exchequer Chamber The Court (Bramwell, B, Pigott, B, Quain and Archibald, JJ, and Amphlett, B) were divided in opinion Those who thought that the relation of bailor and bailee existed "did not, however, think that it necessarily followed, under the circumstances, that the bailment involved a warranty that the horse bailed was fit for the purpose for which he was bailed, but thought that the plaintiff might have taken on himself the risk with respect to his fitness, and that the case on appeal stated the facts so imperfectly as to this latter question that the only course under the circumstances was to order a new trial in order that it might be submitted to a jury"

Accordingly, there was a new trial, when the jury came substantially to the same conclusion, and assessed the same damages They found as facts that the horse was not reasonably fit to be driven in a hansom cab, that the defendant did not take reasonable precautions to supply the plaintiff with a reasonably fit horse, that the plaintiff did not take upon himself the risk of the horse being reasonably fit, and that the horse and cab were entrusted to the plaintiff as bailee and not as servant. The Court of Common Pleas (Coleridge, C J, Keating, Brett, and Grove, JJ) unanimously refused to disturb the verdict (L R, 10 C P 92).

Cockburn, C J, in *Venables v Smith*, agreed to a certain extent "with the reasoning of the majority of the Court" in *Fowler v Lock*.

In *Venables v Smith* (2 Q B D 279), 1877, Cockburn, C J, said —

"I agree that, independently of the Acts of Parliament relating to this subject, the relation between them would be that of bailor and bailee, not that of master and servant. But I think that the provisions of the Acts of Parliament alter what would otherwise be the relation of the proprietor and driver, and for the protection of the public produce the result that, as regards mischief done by the driver, who is selected by the proprietor, the relation of master and servant so far exists as to render the proprietor responsible for the acts of the driver."

There the whole question was whether the driver, who was drunk and driving furiously at the moment of running over the plaintiff, was acting within the scope of his employment, and it was held that he was. At the moment he was on the way back to the proprietor's stables, but at the end of the mews in which they were he drove to a tobacconist's a little way off, and the accident happened on his return.

The question as to whether or not a driver is acting within the scope of his employment received a striking commentary in *Mann v Ward* (8 T L R 699), 1892. There a cab belonging to the defendant, which was being driven by an unlicensed person who was drunk, and not his servant, while the licensed driver was drunk inside, knocked down and injured the plaintiff. At the trial the Judge nonsuited him, and the Court of Appeal unanimously held that he was right, Lord Esher, M R, remarking "A man was only liable for the negligence of his servant in the course of his employment and who has caused an injury. The master was not liable for the negligence of his driver, for he did not cause the injury, nor for the negligence of the other, because he was not his servant." "How can it be said," said Bowen, L J, "that it was the natural consequence of the defendant's driver being drunk that another man should get on the box and drive?" But this case was very severely handled by the Court of Appeal in *Engelhart v Farren* ([1897], 1 Q B 240).

Poules v Hider was considered in *King v. Spurr* (8 Q B D 104), 1881. That was a case of injury caused to the plaintiff's cart and pony through the negligence of a London cabdriver, who hired it from the defendant, the proprietor, at a weekly payment, but himself supplied the horse, harness, and whip. In the County Court the plaintiff was non-suited on the ground that there was no evidence that the driver was the defendant's servant. Grove, J., cited the last sentence from Lord Campbell's judgment, above, and proceeded :—

"We [i.e. Bowen and Grove, JJ.] do not take so wide a view of the operation of these Acts as Lord Campbell does, and the part of his judgment which holds that the proprietor must be taken to receive the earnings of the cab, suggests that he was applying to the case the common law relation of the parties. Here the facts do not admit any contention that at common law the relation of master and servant existed, and I doubt whether the Court in *Powles v. Hider* would have decided as they did if they had had before them as a fact that the cabdriver was not in the service of the proprietor." The learned judge then pointed out that Sections 21, 28, and 35 of the Act of 1843 "are consistent with the non existence of the relation of master and servant [1]. If the Metropolitan Carriage Acts intended in all cases to make the proprietor responsible for the driver, as a master for his servant, this could have been done in a sentence, and an enactment making him liable in summary proceedings would have been differently worded and have only fixed the limit. *Venables v. Smith* throws no additional light upon the question, for it proceeded entirely upon *Powles v. Hider*."

Bowen, J., remarked "Putting statutes aside, the relation in this case of the proprietor and driver of the cab would be simply that of bailor and bailee. Ought we to say that the learned judge below is wrong in holding such still to be their true relation, the Act of Parliament notwithstanding? Only—so it seems to me—if, as a matter of law, the Act of Parliament of necessity and under all circumstances has created between proprietor and driver the

---

[1] "S. 28 was much relied on by the counsel for the plaintiff. It was contended that this constituted a statutory liability to the extent of £10, and therefore a relation of master and servant. But, on the other hand, it seems plain that this is intended only to provide a summary mode of obtaining compensation, and it may be said if the Act intended to create such a relation why should it limit the liability? This section tends to show that the Act did not contemplate that relation, but only created a kind of guarantee in case the owner should abscond or not pay." (51 L. J. Rep., Q. B. 107)

relation of master and servant. Has the Act of Parliament done so in express terms? No. Has it done so by necessary implication? To hold this would be to read a new section into, and engraft it upon, the Act. It is true that the Act of Parliament uses in several places the terms 'service' and 'employment,' but it uses them, I think, as sufficiently descriptive, for the purposes only of the construction of the Act, of the relation of the two persons, and not with the object of enacting that, for all purposes outside the Act, such is to be always their relation. And, indeed, in many cases the effect of the Act, taken in connection with the circumstances, is in my opinion to bring about this very relation. I go further, I think that there is a *primâ facie* presumption that such is their relation, in consequence of the respective positions in which the Act of Parliament has placed the proprietor on the one hand and the driver on the other. But to say that in all circumstances the Act of Parliament, as a matter of law, necessarily creates such a relation, is to go, in my opinion, too far, and to make Acts of Parliament, not to interpret them. Lord Campbell [in *Powles v Hider*] and Cockburn, C J [in *Venables v Smith*], do, in my opinion, employ language which puts forward this proposition in its extreme form. Upon consideration I think that we are not disregarding their judgments, but only qualifying the expressions with which they have accompanied their judgments in holding that the proprietor in this case was not liable." (But see p 73)

In 1889 in *King v London Improved Cab Company, Limited* (23 Q B D 281), the Court of Appeal (Lord Esher, M R, Lindley, L J, and Lopes, L J) upheld *Venables v Smith*, and to a certain extent the view of Willes, J, in *Fowler v Lock* (i e in so far as the relation of owner and driver affects third parties) Here, the driver paid so much a day for horse and cab, the engagement was for the day, without necessity of notice on either side. The defendants had no control over the driver. The action was for personal injuries through negligent driving. I have come to the conclusion," says Lord Esher, M R, "that the defendants are liable. In my opinion the agreement proved to have been made between them and the driver did not constitute the latter their servant. It seems to me that the agreement did not give to the proprietor such control as he would have over a servant. Further, I do not consider that the cases decided as to the hiring of a cab will conclude this case, which arises between a stranger who has not hired the cab and the proprietor, and[1] even if the judgment of Lord Campbell in *Powles v Hider* might be supported, as has been suggested, on the ground that there the cab proprietor held out the driver as his servant to persons hiring the cab, I do not think that there can be said to be

---

[1] The rest of this sentence and the next sentence are taken from the report in 58 L J, N S, Q B 158

holding out by the proprietor as regards strangers In my opinion, therefore, the question which we have to determine turns altogether upon the true construction of the statute 6-7 V 86 Without going in detail through the sections of the Act, it seems to me to be a necessary implication arising from them that the Act was made in favour of the public irrespective of the agreement that might subsist between the proprietor and the driver," and he concluded that, *so far as the public are concerned*, the relation of master and servant must be deemed to exist Lindley, L J, appears in this case to have his suspicions of *King v. Spurr*

In *Keen v Henry* ([1894] 1 Q B 292), the plaintiff recovered damages from the defendant, the proprietor of a cab, which, through the negligent driving of the cabman, as the jury found, ran into and killed a mare belonging to the plaintiff, Lawrence, J, holding that *King v Spurr* had been overruled by the Court of Appeal in *King v London Improved Cab Company* Here the defendant had let the cab "without horses or harness" to his son for a term of three months on a weekly tenancy As the hirer or his servants had the sole charge or custody of the cab, it was agreed that he should indemnify the owner against all risks, loss, &c, and against all claims for injuries arising through the carelessness or wilful misbehaviour of the hirer or his servants The negligent driver was engaged by the son The Court (Esher, M R., Lopes, L J, and Kay, L J.) unanimously upheld the judge below "In such a case," said the former, "the Act [6-7 V 86] gives the plaintiff a right of action against the defendant, although the driver is not his servant This right, however, does not interfere with any right of action which the plaintiff may have at common law against the driver's master in the ordinary sense of that word The proprietors of hackney carriages cannot, by letting their carriages, escape from their liability under the statute," adding later "it must be understood that we are all of opinion that *King v Spurr* has been overruled"

Keen v Henry, it will be noticed, is an extreme case of the proprietor's liability, for he did nothing but supply the cab, having nothing to do with the driver.

In the two cases just cited it would have been an advantage if the Court of Appeal had indicated the sections in the Act of 1843 which compelled it to the conclusion that since that statute the relation of master and servant was deemed to exist between proprietor and driver as against third parties As the matter stands, it must be taken to be the view of the Court of Appeal that there is a general "implication" in the Act to this effect Lord Campbell, however, in his judgment in *Powles v Hider*, does point to the sections which led him to his decision, and so does Grove, J, in a contrary sense, in *King v Spurr*

It is now, therefore, settled law that as regards third parties, proprietor and driver are master and servant. As regards one another they may either be bailor and bailee or master and servant, according to the terms of their contract

That contract is usually[1] for the use of a cab and a change of horses at so much per day. Consequently the state of things disclosed in *Milson v Silvester* (above, p 68) no longer generally exists, the proprietor has no control over the driver while he is "out." In this respect, therefore there is no relation of master and servant. It is clearly one of bailor or bailee at common law. Consequently "where a man hires a horse and carriage, there is an implied obligation on his part arising out of the contract to return them in the condition in which he received them, fair wear and tear and certain accidents excepted" (*per* Cave and Charles, JJ, *The Coupé Company v Maddick* [1891], 2 Q B at 415)

RELATIONS BETWEEN THE AUTHORITIES AND PROPRIETORS AND DRIVERS.

1. *PROPRIETORS.*

See pp 36-43 for certain penalties

"Proprietor" is defined as "every person who, either alone or in partnership with any other person, shall keep any hackney carriage . . . . or who shall be concerned otherwise than as a driver or attendant in employing for hire any hackney carriage" (6-7 V 86, 2).

A proprietor is liable to pay any sum inflicted by way of penalty, compensation, or costs on his driver under the Hackney Carriage Acts of 1831, 1843, and 1853, and the Prevention of Cruelty to Animals Act

---

[1] The terms are now largely regulated by the Asquith Award, for which see Appendix E

of 1849 As to the relation of the three first mentioned of these statutes see p. 30.

A proprietor must take out a police licence for each cab.

A duty of this sort is at least as old as 9 A. 23 (1710) It was re-enacted in 1831 by 1-2 W. IV. 22, 2, which was repealed in 1869 by 32-3 V 14, 39 It is now imposed by 32-3 V 115, 6 (where for "revision or suspension" no doubt "revocation or suspension" is to be read) and s 7, and regulated by the Secretary of State's Order made in pursuance of s 6 (see below)

The licence, if not revoked or suspended, is in force for a year (ss. 6 and 10)

By an Order of 18th August, 1897, which came into force on 1st September, 1897, the Secretary of State has made the following rules [1] with respect to such licences under his statutory power :—

1 A licence may be granted to any person by the Commissioner of Police of the Metropolis [Section 11 of the Act] subject to the following exceptions —

(A) A licence shall not be granted to any person under the age of twenty-one years, or to any person who shall have been previously convicted of felony, and any licence so granted shall be void

(B) The Commissioner may at his discretion refuse a licence to any person who has been convicted of a misdemeanour or of cruelty to animals, or who, having previously held a licence for a hackney or a stage carriage, has had such previous licence revoked or suspended

[No doubt the Commissioner could refuse a cab licence to one whose previous stage carriage licence had been thus dealt with or vice versâ (but see note to Rule 15 (II) below)]

2 A person desirous of obtaining a licence shall make application at the office of the Commissioner [2]

3 The price of a licence is £2 [It must not exceed £2 2s 32-3 V 115, 6 (1)]

---

[1] The text of the Order is here and below (p 83) abbreviated

[2] It has not been thought necessary to reprint here the various forms under this Order given in the schedules

4. The £2 must be paid with the application.

5. The application is to be returned to the applicant with a receipt for the £2.

6. The applicant must then bring the cab to be licensed to the police station of the district for examination by the Inspector of Public Carriages, delivering to him at the same time the application and receipt. The Inspector, if he shall find such cab fit for public use, shall cause the number plate—a metal plate, bearing the number which is to distinguish that cab—to be affixed thereto in his presence, together with such approval mark as the Commissioner may from time to time direct, and shall sign a certificate. The number plate is to be set on the back of a four-wheeler, and in the spring block on the back under the driver's seat in a hansom, and in both there is to be one inside.

9. The Form of the Licence. It determines the number of persons to be carried inside and outside according to the Inspector's certificate. That number the proprietor must paint outside on the back of his cab [Clause 19 of this Order, pursuant to 32-3 V. 115, 9 (1)].

10. An application for a licence on behalf of any co-partnership or company shall be made by and issued to the senior partner or secretary or manager of the company, who shall be responsible for the observance of its conditions and liable to all penalties for breaches of them, as if he were the person solely interested in the licence.

11. In the case of the death of any proprietor during the currency of his licence it may be brought to the Commissioner, who may, by endorsement on it, transfer it to the personal representatives of the deceased, or to his widow, or child, if such child is of age. Similarly on the marriage of a female proprietor the licence may be transferred to her husband. In a company it may be transferred from the secretary or manager to his successor.

[The insertion of the last sentence is due to *Hodges v. The London Tramways and Omnibus Company* (12 Q.B.D. 105), 1883, *i.e.* before this rule existed. The plaintiff was manager of the defendant company, and thus became the licensee of their vehicles. When he ceased to be manager he desired to surrender the licences, and tendered them to the Commissioner, who refused to accept them on the ground that he had not complied with 2-3 W. IV. 120, 14 (which relates to stage carriages) by not delivering up certain numbered plates (no longer in his possession). The Court of Queen's Bench granted him an injunction to restrain the company from using his name on their number plates, there being then no provision for transferring a licence from one manager to another]

12 The following are the conditions upon which the licence is issued —

(A) The proprietor shall not permit or suffer the cab to be sublet

(B) If he changes his address he must within seven days get the Commissioner to erase the old and endorse the new one The unerased address is the legal one for all licensing purposes [see 1 & 2 W IV 22, 68]

(C) The proprietor —

 (1) Shall not knowingly permit his cab to be used for an illegal purpose

 (2) Shall not erase or deface his licence

 (3) Shall at all times, when required, produce his licence to the Commissioner

 (4) Shall at all reasonable times allow the Inspectors of public carriages free access to his premises and stables to inspect his licensed cabs, the horses of those cabs, and their harness

 (5) Shall, within three days after notice, deliver up his licence to the Inspector of public carriages at the police station of the district of his address, and bring his cab thither to have the plates unfixed and given up to the Inspector

(D) He must not conceal or remove any of the plates or alter or obliterate any number or mark put on the cab by the Commissioner's authority, and he shall not allow anyone to do any of these things except by that authority [30-1 V 134, 17 (2), see Penalty No 24]

(E) He must keep the cab and all its furniture and appointments and the horse's harness in perfect order and repair, and shall not suffer any printed, written, or other matter to appear outside or inside the cab by way of advertisement, unless approved by the Commissioner

(F) The proprietor of a cab propelled by mechanical means shall not employ as a driver thereof anyone who is not specially licensed therefor

[This sub section and (G)— not here relevant—and (H) appear for the first time in a Secretary of State's Order The form of licence for a motor cabman is given in a schedule, but is not reproduced here. Both in the case of carriages drawn by animal power, and of those propelled by mechanical power, the licence is to act as driver of one sort "and none other"]

 (ii) The proprietor of a cab drawn by animal power shall not employ as a driver thereof anyone who only has a licence to drive motor cabs

13. The proprietor must, within three days after his licence expires, deliver it up to the Inspector at the police station, and bring the cab there so that the number plate may be unfixed and delivered up to the Inspector

14. Any licence erased or defaced shall be void

15. The licence may be revoked or suspended—

 (i) If the proprietor fails to comply with the conditions prescribed in s 12 above

 (ii) In any of the events in which it might have been revoked or suspended at the time of the passing of the Act of 1869

[See Penalties Nos 17 and 37 (pp 38, 41)]

It is hoped that all these "events" have been enumerated above (pp 36-43) or below (p 81) 6-7 V 86, 26, supplies an instance where a proprietor's licence was revocable, but the section was repealed shortly before the passing of the Act of 1869 by 32-3 V 14, 39

From some words of this sub-section here omitted it might conceivably be inferred that the penalty ensues in any of the events in which a stage carriage licence could have been revoked or suspended, as well as those in which a cab licence could, for the Order throughout deals with both classes of public carriages. But only cabs are dealt with in this book, and it is safe to assume that under this sub-section a cab licence is only to be revoked &c where a cab licence could be revoked &c before 1869, and similarly (but not interchangeably) a stage carriage licence where that could have been revoked &c before 1869

 (iii) If the proprietor commits a breach of the said Act, or of this Order, or is convicted of felony or a misdemeanour

The notice issued by the Commissioner to Proprietors is printed in Appendix C

He must take out annually an excise licence for each non-motor cab; this duty, otherwise called the Wheel Tax, is fifteen shillings. This licence runs from

1st January to 31st December, but if taken out on or after 1st October the duty, in the case of a hansom or of a four-wheeler weighing less than 4 cwt., is seven shillings and sixpence (47-8 V. 25, 3, 4)

As to this tax, a witness told the Committee of Enquiry that it was " agreed by all parties who know anything at all about the matter, that it was never intended that we should pay that tax, but, having started with it, we have been fixed with it ever since, and my own opinion is that it was never legalised until 1884" (*Blue Book*, 6720). The Committee recommended the abolition of the tax (*Report*, p 10) It goes now to the London County Council (51-2 V 41, 20 (1))

The excise duty on motor cabs (liable under 51 V 8, see p. 11) is, if its weight exceeds one ton unladen, but does not exceed two tons unladen, two guineas, and, in all other cases, three guineas. "Every such duty shall be paid together with the duty on the licence for the locomotive as a carriage or a hackney carriage" (59-60 V. 36, 8 (1) and (2)).

It may be added that cabs "are allowed to have armorial bearings on the panels free from tax, and servants employed by a licensed keeper of hackney carriages to drive the carriages or take care of the horses are not charged as taxable servants" (3 *Dowell's History of Taxation*, 45).

While the driver remains in his service he must keep his licence (6-7 V 86, 21) Penalty £3

He must enter thereon his own name and address and the days on which the driver enters and quits his service respectively (*ibid.* s 8).

The language of the section is peremptory, but no penalty is denounced for disobedience in this Act But according to the view so often taken here, the effect of 16-7 V 86 is that there is a penalty of 40s. for any omission (see p 30)

These entries must be *bonâ fide*. If the proprietor enters one date of one employment, where there have been several, he ought to enter the others too (*per* Lawrance, J., and Kennedy, J., in *Norris v. Birch*, below, p. 88).

"Chair-marking" (see p. 87) is a defacement within this section, which says: "In case any of the particulars entered or endorsed upon any licence in pursuance of this Act shall be erased or defaced, every such licence shall be wholly void and of none effect," and the driver, the owner of the licence, has an action against the proprietor, either in the High Court (as in *Hurrell v Ellis*, 2 C B 295, in 1845, or *Rogers v. Macnamara*, 14 C B. 27, in 1853), or he may obtain compensation under Section 22 of the Act of 1843 from a magistrate (as in *Norris v. Birch* in 1895)

The proprietor must not knowingly allow anyone in his employ without a licence to drive, but if he can prove "unavoidable necessity," he will be excused if he does not employ such person for more than twenty-four hours (6-7 V 86, 10).

He must produce his driver's licence when he has to produce the latter before a justice, if he is still in his service (*ibid.* s. 10).

When the latter leaves his service, he must deliver up the licence on demand under pain of paying compensation for the delay, unless he has some complaint to make against him before a justice, in which case he has twenty-four hours to make it in under the same pain. He must deposit the licence with the clerk to the justice (*ibid.* 24).

He may be summoned to produce a driver charged with any offence under the Acts of 1831, 1843, and 1853 (the first), or that of 1849 for the Prevention of Cruelty to Animals. The penalty for failure to do so is forty shillings (6-7 V. 86, 35; 16-7 V. 33, 21; 12-3 V. 92, 22).

Where there are more proprietors than one, only one need be named in proceedings (6-7 V. 86, 44).

He must not let his cab or horses after notice from the Commissioner of Police that either of them is "unfit for public use" on pain of his licence being suspended (16-7 V. 33, 2).

He must not allow any bill or advertisement &c. to obstruct the light or ventilation (*ibid.* s. 15; Secretary of State's Order, 12 (E)).

He must not withdraw a licensed cab from hire for two consecutive days, and for any two days in one week, "without just cause," unless he gives ten days' notice to the Commissioner of Police. Penalty, twenty shillings a day in respect of each cab, and revocation or suspension of licence (16-7 V. 127, 16).

Horses and cabs may be seized in a public highway under 45-6 V. 43, 13, The Bills of Sale Act (1878) Amendment Act, 1882, and in the absence of actual damage arising from the removal within the five days, no action will lie (*O'Neil v City and County Finance Co*, 17 Q B D. 234, in 1886)

2. DRIVERS.

LICENCES

The following return was made by New Scotland Yard to the Committee of Enquiry in 1894 (*Blue Book*, p 301) :—

The requirements of the Licensing Authority in granting drivers' licences in regard to (A) character, (B) knowledge of London, (C) practice in driving

> (A) The requirements are set forth in the certificate on the requisition form It shows that the applicant must be sober, honest, and of good character, must be a skilful driver and humane in the treatment of horses The certificate is required to be signed by two householders who have had a personal knowledge of the applicant for the past three years The form has also to be signed by the last employer Inquiry is then made by the police
>
> (B) Applicants for licences are examined by an officer (usually the chief inspector) as to their knowledge of the principal routes to and from railway stations squares, theatres, public buildings, &c &c and certificates of fitness are not signed until applicants have acquired such knowledge
>
> (C) Provision is made in the form of requisition for a certificate to be signed by some householder or other responsible person who has a knowledge of an applicant's capabilities as a driver

Formerly the driver had to take out a licence under 6-7 V. 86, 8, 10 It was granted by the Registrar of Metropolitan Public Carriages, whose office was abolished and whose duties were transferred in 1850 to the Commissioners of Police for the Metropolis (13-4 V 7) There is now only one such Commissioner

(19-20 V 2, 1). The Commissioner for the City of London is appointed by virtue of 2-3 V. 94, 3, but he has nothing to do with the licensing of cabs (*Blue Book*, 5487).

A driver must now take out the licence under 32-3 V. 115, 8, which, if it is not revoked or suspended, remains in force for a year.

In pursuance of that section the last Order of the Secretary of State on the subject provided as follows —

> 16 Licences to act as driver of a cab may be granted by the Commissioner, provided that the applicant be not less than twenty one years of age
>
> 17 Licences so granted shall be respectively in the forms contained in the Schedules [not here printed] For each licence Five Shillings must be paid to the Receiver of the Metropolitan Police

This sum is the maximum allowed by s 8 Clause 18 is set out above p 35 The note to Clause 15 (ii) of the Order (p 78) applies here

In this connection *Reg v. Commissioners of Police* (5 B & S 585, 12 W R 983, 10 L T, N S 573, 10 Jur N. S 1254, 28 J P 438) 1864, is very important. "This was an application for a *mandamus* to the Commissioners of the Metropolitan Police to grant a licence to a conductor of an omnibus under 6-7 V 86 The applicant had been a licensed omnibus conductor for eight years, and his licence expired on the 1st June last He had made the usual application for the renewal of his licence, and produced to the Commissioners of Police the certificate of good behaviour required by Section 8 of the Statute . . The applicant was informed at the office of the Commissioners that his licence was suspended for a month, and would not be granted until 1st July The ground of suspension was that the applicant had been summoned before the magistrates three times, and fined on each occasion" The Court of Queen's Bench (Cockburn, C J, Crompton, Mellor, and Shee, JJ) unanimously refused the application, the former saying 'The jurisdiction exercised by the Commissioners of Police is essential to the preservation of proper conduct in these men It is quite clear that the Commissioners are not bound to be satisfied with the mere production of a certificate of good behaviour, but are entitled to be satisfied that the conduct of the bearer has been proper. That appears to be so from the provisions of s. 14. Therefore, when it was disclosed that this applicant had been three times fined, it was competent to the Commissioners to say that they would not grant him a licence, notwithstanding s. 8. If, then, they could refuse the licence altogether, it was perfectly competent for them to say to the applicant that what he had done during the last year was a sufficient reason why they should not at once grant him a licence, and that as a salutary check they would withhold it until 1st July, and that if he returned for it at that period they would give it to him."

With regard to the vexed question of the desirability of restricting the number of drivers' licences, legislation would be necessary to effect this end. This, apparently, is the view of the Home Office (*Blue Book*, 9,250), which, however, probably only means that no Minister would take upon himself the responsibility of initiating a system of restriction, and so promoting a monopoly. It is probable that a *mandamus* would lie either to the Secretary of State or to the Commissioner to compel him to grant a licence, or at any rate to receive and adjudicate upon any particular application, if either of them had declined to do so solely on the ground that there were already too many licences in existence for the public convenience. The Act says: "A licence may be granted at such price, on such conditions, be in such form . . . . and, generally, be dealt with in such manner as the said Secretary of State may by order prescribe &c." (s. 8). Could the words "on such conditions" include a stipulation that a given licence should not come into force until the total number in existence had fallen to a certain limit? If they could, the *legal* difficulty in curtailing the number of licences disappears.

The driver at the time of the granting of his licence, is entitled to receive an Abstract of the Cab Laws and Penalties [1] then in force, and a metal ticket with a number corresponding to that of his licence, and a new one when the old one is worn out, at a price not more than three shillings (6-7 V. 86, 9, 19).

The police are empowered to summarily arrest anyone "unlawfully acting as a driver"—*e g.* without the proprietor's consent (see p 40)—and also "if necessary," to take charge of the cab and horse and to place them in safety till the proprietor can apply for them (6-7 V. 86, 27)

The place of safe custody in which, generally, when the police arrest a driver, the horse and cab are put is known as "the greenyard"—originally no doubt a "pound" Usually it is a livery stable with the owner of which the police have an arrangement as to charges. It is legally recognised by 1-2 W. IV. 23, 60.

3. *THE RELATIONS BETWEEN DRIVERS AND PROPRIETORS.*

See generally 1 and 2 preceding and pp 66–74 for the presumptions of law.

In certain cases (see p. 81), the proprietor may be summoned to produce a driver when the latter is charged with an offence

---

[1] The book may be obtained from Messrs Eyre & Spottiswoode, price 4d

Sir John Bridge informed the Committee of Enquiry—

"It is the universal practice to summon the proprietor to produce the driver in all cases for offences to which the 35th section of 6 & 7 Vict [Will IV is a misprint] c 86 is applicable [for this section see p. 81] Under the statute I think the magistrate has a discretion to summon the driver, but this is never done when the proprietor can be summoned. If the practice were otherwise many offenders would escape punishment and the public would not have the protection which is afforded them by the present practice" (*Blue Book*, p 262, note)

Where the proprietor has had to pay fines or costs incurred by his driver (see p. 74), he may recover the same from the latter under a magistrate's order, if need be, by distress and sale of his goods, and, if the distress does not yield enough, the magistrate may send the driver to prison with or without hard labour, until the sum due is paid or for any term not exceeding two months (1-2 W IV. 28, 6-7 V 86, 35). The same procedure applies to "compensation" which the driver is ordered to pay (see p 39), but for the present practice see p. 90.

Magistrates may hear and determine—

> Disputes between proprietors and drivers on all matters of complaint,

And may order to either party the payment of any sum as—

> Wages, or
>
> Earnings in respect of the cab, or
>
> On account of any deposit of money;

And may order "compensation to the proprietor"—

> In respect of damage or loss which shall have arisen through the neglect or default of any driver to the property of his employer entrusted to his care (see p. 74), or

> In respect of any sum which the proprietor has actually paid under a magistrate's order on account of the driver's negligence or wilful misconduct (see p. 74);

And they may order—

> Compensation to either party in respect of any other matter of complaint between them.

But as to "earnings," the proprietor cannot recover in this way, unless under an agreement in writing signed by the driver in the presence of a competent witness—which agreement does not require a stamp—but it seems that a driver might recover in respect of "earnings" whether he had signed such an agreement or not (6-7 V. 86, 22, 23). Imprisonment in default of payment in the above cases of "wages," "earnings," or "deposit" cannot be for more than a month without hard labour (*ibid.*, s 39; but see p. 34).

"Chairmarking" is within the words "any other matter of complaint between them" (*per* Lawrance, J., in *Norris v. Birch* [1895], 1 Q. B. 639).

> A driver informed the Committee of Enquiry that "chairmarking" is "entering a date when a driver starts work for an employer, and

when he is discharged or leaves, in some peculiar manner which indicates to another proprietor that he has done something wrong, and is not to be employed" (*Blue Book*, 3,771)

It cannot be said that every form of this practice is illegal.

The relevant words of Section 8 are—

"On every licence of a driver the registrar shall cause proper columns to be prepared, in which every proprietor employing the driver .. named in such licence shall enter his own name and address and the day on which such driver shall enter into and shall quit his service respectively"

In *Norris v Birch* Lawrance, J, seems to think that where there has been more than one employment, one—at any rate the last—complete entry of dates, both of entering and quitting, is a sufficient compliance with the section, and Kennedy, J, says "We have not to deal with a case where the entry, if correctly stated, requires the insertion of two dates, and one of them is omitted. I am not prepared to say that if that were the case, and people chose to treat such a state of things as a bad mark, there would have been a defacing of the licence" The learned judge, if he is correctly reported, apparently means that a mere omission would not be a defacement, and that the omission *in this case* was not a violation of the section, as there was one complete entry For, if there is not at least one complete entry, there is a clear violation of the section

N B —Neither learned judge lays it down that whenever there is an entry of entering there must be one of quitting, and *vice versâ*

The true rule seems to be that any writing or mark upon the licence which is not a genuine compliance with the statute for the purposes thereof is a defacement (*Hurrell v Ellis*, 2 C B 295, in 1845, where the proprietor had written on the licence a strong attack on the holder's fitness to drive) This case was quoted with approval in *Rogers v Macnamara* (14 C B 27, in 1853) There a proprietor, in returning an omnibus conductor's licence, had written on it, "Discharged for being 1s 4d short, A.M"—a statement which he pleaded was true But it was held that an action would lie against him under 6 7 V 86, 8, Jervis, C J, remarking "Now unless the act charged can be said to be justified by some moral duty on the defendant—which can hardly be seriously contended—the action is clearly maintainable Under no circumstances can the employer be justified in taking upon himself to adjudicate on his own complaint by writing on the licence that which the Act of Parliament authorises the justice alone to endorse" (see p 35) This is a strong case because plaintiff's counsel admitted that defendant might have had redress for the alleged embezzlement from a justice, who could then have endorsed the conviction. But as a learned judge pointed out, the plaintiff's offence could only affect the question of damages in the action.

"The only person who has authority to make an endorsement on the driver's licence is the magistrate, when the party is brought before him charged with an offence" (*per* Erle, C. J., in *Heather v. Brewer* 15 C. B., N. S. 805, in 1864).

When a driver leaves the service of a proprietor (see p. 80), if the latter do not deliver up the licence of the former to him within the proper time (generally twenty-four hours), the former may summon the latter and get "reasonable" compensation and his licence back by the magistrate's order, unless he revokes or suspends the licence for misconduct (6-7 V. 86, 24).

When a proprietor is summoned to produce a driver in court, the latter is entitled to notice (as to time and place &c.) from the former, at the address specified in the licence, or, if the proprietor has it not, at his usual abode (*ibid* 35).

PROCEDURE.

Speaking generally, all proceedings under the cab laws are begun by a summons (see pp. 31-46). The occasions on which an action must be brought in the County Court or the High Court are rare, and need not be considered here.

Historically, a Metropolitan Police Office was created in 1831 by 1-2 W. IV. 22, 62, for the trial of London cab cases, without however, such jurisdiction as magistrates sitting elsewhere possessed being taken away.[1] The Act of 1843 confirmed this state of things (see, for instance 6-7 V. 86, 36, side by side with s. 39) The institution of a special office was, however, permissive and not compulsory, and apparently not being very successful was quietly allowed to fall into desuetude.

The magistrate may in the first instance, instead of summoning the proprietor (see pp 85, 86), issue his summons direct to the driver, or even his warrant for his apprehension (6-7 V 86, 41)

If the proprietor is summoned, the driver may be convicted, even in his absence (s 35), if the offence charged is one for which he has no right to be tried by a jury. In such cases the magistrate must be satisfied that he has been served with the summons. For this purpose his address is that specified in his licence, unless it has expired, when his address is his usual place of abode (*ibid* 41) If, despite the notice, he do not attend, a warrant may be issued.

---

[1] The Assistant Commissioner of the Metropolitan Police told the Committee of Enquiry in 1894 that he believed there was " a Court which used to sit in Essex Street to try cab cases more than forty years ago" (*Blue Book*, 603) See *Cloud v Turfery*, 2 Bing at p 320.

This seems to be the effect of Section 35 which is somewhat confusingly drawn

For the proprietor's remedy when he has had to pay any fine &c. inflicted on his driver see p. 74.

It is, perhaps, worth noting that actions and prosecutions for anything "done in pursuance or under the authority" of the Acts of 1831 and 1843 were formerly subject to a special procedure (regulated by 1-2 W IV 22, 73, or 6-7 V 86, 47), but both these sections were repealed in 1893 by The Public Authorities Protection Act (56-7 V 6, 1, Schedule) And now it is provided by this Act —

"The action, prosecution, or proceeding [against persons acting in execution of statutory or other public duty] shall not lie or be instituted unless it is commenced within six months next after the act, neglect, or default complained of, or in case of a continuance of injury or damage, within six months next after ceasing thereof" (s. 1 (a))

Appeal

In the Metropolitan Police District—where there is a greater right of appeal from a Police Court than elsewhere—in every case of summary order or conviction by a stipendiary magistrate or two Justices in Special or Petty Sessions of the Peace, where a penalty or sum of more than three pounds is ordered to be paid or imprisonment for more than a calendar month is ordered, the defendant may appeal to the next Quarter Sessions (2-3 V. 71, 50; 3-4 V 84, 6).

Speaking generally, there is no appeal from a Court of summary jurisdiction except where a sentence of imprisonment, without the option of a fine, is passed on a person who has not pleaded guilty, and not then if the imprisonment is inflicted for failure to comply with an order for the payment of money, for the finding of sureties, for the entering into any recognisance, or for the giving of any security The appeal is to Quarter Sessions (42-3 V 49, 19).

On a point of law the magistrate may state a case for the consideration of the High Court.

APPENDIX A.

PLACES IN THE METROPOLITAN POLICE DISTRICT NOT IN MIDDLESEX

In Essex

Barking (Town, Chadwell, Great Ilford, and Ripple Wards), Chigwell, Chingford, Dagenham, East Ham, West Ham (Church Street, Plaistow, and Stratford Wards), Little Ilford, Loughton, Low Leyton Waltham Abbey and Town (Hamlets of Holyfield, Sewardstone, and Upshire), Walthamstow, Wanstead, and Woodford

In Kent.

Beckenham, Bexley, Bromley, Charlton, Chiselhurst, Crayford, Down, Eltham, Erith, Farnborough, Foot's Cray, Greenwich, Hayes, Keston, Kidbrooke (Liberty of), Lee, Lewisham, Mottingham (Hamlet of), Northcray, Orpington, Plumstead, St Mary's Cray, Deptford (St Nicholas and St Paul), St Paul's Cray, Wickham East, Wickham West, and Woolwich

In Surrey

Addington, Banstead, Barnes, Battersea, Beddington, Bermondsey, Camberwell, Carshalton, Cheam, Chessington, Christchurch, Clapham (Clink Liberty), Coulsdon, Croydon, Cuddington, Epsom, Ewell (Worcester Park), Fartey, Ham with Hatch (Hamlet of), Hatcham (Hamlet of), Hook (Hamlet of), Kew, Kingston-on-Thames, Lambeth, Long Ditton, Maldon, Merton, Mitcham, Mordon, Mortlake, Moulsey East, Moulsey West, Newington, Penge (Hamlet of), Petersham,

PLACES IN METROPOLITAN POLICE DISTRICT NOT IN MIDDLESEX

Putney (Roehampton), Richmond, Rotherhithe, Sanderstead, Southwark (St. George, St John, St Olave, St Saviour, St Thomas), Streatham, Sutton, Thames Ditton (Hamlets of Claygate, Ember, and Weston), Tooting, Wallington (Hamlet of), Wandsworth, Warlingham, Wimbledon, and Woodmansterne

In Herts

Aldenham (Hamlet of St Theobald), Barnet East, Bushey, Cheshunt, Chipping Barnet, Elstree, Northaw, Ridge, Shenley, and Totteridge

APPENDIX B.

NOTICE TO DRIVERS OF HACKNEY CARRIAGES.

Complaints having been received by the Commissioner of Police that hansom cabs frequently carry as luggage such large trunks and packages as to render it impossible for the drivers to have an uninterrupted view of the roadway and a proper control of their horses, and that accidents—one of which was fatal—have been thereby caused,

The Commissioner feels it his duty to point out to drivers that the construction of hansom cabs does not admit of anything but small packages being carried on the roofs with safety, and that the practice complained of is most dangerous, and he has to inform drivers that any further similar complaints received will be very seriously considered before licences are renewed

E R C BRADFORD,
The Commissioner of Police of the Metropolis.

METROPOLITAN POLICE OFFICE,
PUBLIC CARRIAGE BRANCH,
August, 1894

APPENDIX C.

NOTICE TO PROPRIETORS OF HACKNEY CARRIAGES AS TO CONDITIONS FOR OBTAINING A CERTIFICATE OF FITNESS.

Hackney Carriages must be submitted for Inspection in a thoroughly good condition, and no Hackney Carriage will be certified fit for public use unless it is newly painted and varnished. The following conditions must also be strictly complied with

1. That the number of persons to be carried be *distinctly* painted on some part of the back of the carriage

2. That 16 inches at least, measuring in a straight line, are allowed on the seats for each person, and also room for the legs and feet

3. That all hansom cabs, constructed to carry two persons, shall be at least 40 inches in width measuring under each window, and 28 inches from the back of the seat to inside of the door pillar

4. That there is sufficient height inside, not less than 40 inches from the seat to the roof, or in the case of hansom cabs to the window frames, measuring from the top of the cushion

5. That all carriages fitted with noiseless or rubber-tyred wheels have bells affixed either to the carriages, or to the harness of the horse drawing the same.

6. That each four-wheeled carriage has a check-string

7. That straps with holes are placed on the window frames (where considered necessary), and that metal or bone knobs are fixed inside the carriage, to enable the windows to be partially closed

8. That carriages the floors of which are above 18 inches from the ground have steps

9. That an iron frame and chains, or some equally efficient means for securing luggage carried on the roof, are fixed on the outside of all four-wheeled carriages

10. That the floor be covered with rope or coir mats, or some other proper material.

11. That the seats, cushions, &c., are stuffed with horsehair, wool, or flock, and not with hay, straw, seaweed, or whalebone shavings

12. That the doors, windows, seats, roof, springs, wheels, cushions, lining, panels, &c., and all furniture and appointments of the carriage and the harness of the horse or horses used in drawing the same, are in perfect order and repair, the paint and varnish bright and in good condition, and the inside perfectly clean

13. That some effectual remedy be adopted to prevent the rattling of window frames and glasses

14. That no printed, written, or other matter shall appear on the inside or outside of the carriage by way of advertisement.

15. Carriages propelled by mechanical means must comply with the requirements of the Light Locomotives Act (59 & 60 Vict c 36), and of the Regulations of the Local Government Board made in pursuance thereof

16. Proprietors of carriages propelled by mechanical means will be required to furnish a certificate, from an independent firm of engineers, that each carriage submitted for licensing is, so far as the mechanism is concerned, fit for public use

NOTE —Though the above conditions may have been complied with, yet if there be anything in the construction, form, or general appearance which, in the opinion of the Commissioner, renders the carriage unfit for public use, it will not be licensed.

E. R. C. BRADFORD,
The Commissioner of Police of the Metropolis

PUBLIC CARRIAGE OFFICE,
15th March, 1898

The Cost of a Licence to Ply for Hire is Two Pounds.

APPENDIX D.

POLICE NOTICE.

LIGHT LOCOMOTIVES OR MOTOR CARS.

Under the provisions of The Locomotives on Highways Act, 1896 (59 & 60 Vict c 36), the following Regulations dated 9th November, 1896, have been made by the Local Government Board with respect to the use of Light Locomotives on Highways, their construction, and the conditions under which they may be used

ORDER WITH RESPECT TO THE USE OF LIGHT LOCOMOTIVES ON HIGHWAYS.

Article I.—In this Order—

The expression "carriage" includes a waggon, cart, or other vehicle

The expression "horse" includes a mule or other beast of draught or burden, and the expression "cattle" includes sheep

The expression "light locomotive" means a vehicle propelled by mechanical power which is under three tons in weight unladen and is not used for the purpose of drawing more than one vehicle (such vehicle with its locomotive not exceeding in weight unladen four tons), and is so constructed that no smoke or visible vapour is emitted therefrom except from any temporary or accidental cause

In calculating for the purpose of this order the weight of a vehicle unladen, the weight of any water, fuel, or accumulators used for the purpose of propulsion shall not be included

Article II.—No person shall cause or permit a light locomotive to be used on any highway, or shall drive or have charge of a light locomotive when so used, unless the conditions hereinafter set forth shall be satisfied namely—

(1) The light locomotive, if it exceeds in weight unladen five hundredweight, shall be capable of being so worked that it may travel either forwards or backwards.

(2) The light locomotive shall not exceed six and a half feet in width, such width to be measured between its extreme projecting points.

(3) The tyre of each wheel of the light locomotive shall be smooth, and shall, where the same touches the ground, be flat, and of the width following · namely—

(*a*) If the weight of the light locomotive unladen exceeds fifteen hundredweight, but does not exceed one ton, not less than two and a half inches,

(*b*) If such weight exceeds one ton, but does not exceed two tons, not less than three inches,

(*c*) If such weight exceeds two tons, not less than four inches.

Provided that where a pneumatic tyre or other tyre of a soft and elastic material is used, the tyre may be round or curved, and there may be upon the same projections or bosses rising above the surface of the tyre if such projections or bosses are of the same material as that of the tyre itself, or of some other soft and elastic material The width of the tyre shall, for the purpose of this proviso, mean the extreme width of the soft and elastic material on the rim of the wheel when not subject to pressure

(4) The light locomotive shall have two independent brakes in good working order, and of such efficiency that the application of either to such locomotive shall cause two of its wheels on the same axle to be so held that the wheels shall be effectually prevented from revolving, or shall have the same effect in stopping the light locomotive as if such wheels were so held

Provided that in the case of a bicycle this Regulation shall apply as if, instead of two wheels on the same axle, one wheel was therein referred to

(5) The light locomotive shall be so constructed as to admit of its being at all times under such control as not to cause undue interference with passenger or other traffic on any highway

(6) In the case of a light locomotive drawing or constructed to draw another vehicle or constructed or used for the carriage of goods, the name of the owner and the place of his abode or business, and in every such case and in the case of every light locomotive weighing unladen one ton and a half or upwards, the weight of the light locomotive unladen shall be painted in one or more straight lines upon some conspicuous part of the right or off side of the light locomotive in large legible letters in white upon black or black upon white, not less than one inch in height

(7) The light locomotive and all the fittings thereof shall be in such a condition as not to cause, or to be likely to cause, danger to any person on the light locomotive or on any highway.

(8) There shall be in charge of the light locomotive when used on any highway a person competent to control and direct its use and movement

(9) The lamp to be carried attached to the light locomotive in pursuance of Section 2 of the Act shall be so constructed and placed as to exhibit, during the period between one hour after sunset and one hour before sunrise, a white light visible within a reasonable distance in the direction towards which the light locomotive is proceeding or is intended to proceed, and to exhibit a red light so visible in the reverse direction. The lamp shall be placed on the extreme right or off side of the light locomotive in such a position as to be free from all obstruction to the light

> Provided that this Regulation shall not extend to any bicycle, tricycle, or other machine to which Section 85 of The Local Government Act, 1888, applies

Article III.—No person shall cause or permit a light locomotive to be used on any highway for the purpose of drawing any vehicle, or shall drive or have charge of a light locomotive when used for such purpose unless the conditions hereinafter set forth shall be satisfied namely—

    (1) Regulations 2, 3, 5, and 7 of Article II of this Order shall apply as if the vehicle drawn by the light locomotive was therein referred to instead of the light locomotive itself, and Regulation 6 of the Article shall apply as if such vehicle was a light locomotive constructed for the carriage of goods

    (2) The vehicle drawn by the light locomotive, except where the light locomotive travels at a rate not exceeding four miles an hour, shall have a brake in good working order of such efficiency that its application to the vehicle shall cause two of the wheels of the vehicle on the same axle to be so held that the wheels shall be effectually prevented from revolving, or shall have the same effect in stopping the vehicle as if such wheels were so held

    (3) The vehicle drawn by the light locomotive shall, when under the last preceding Regulation a brake is required to be attached thereto, carry upon the vehicle a person competent to apply efficiently the brake Provided that it shall not be necessary to comply with this Regulation if the brakes upon the light locomotive by which the vehicle is drawn are so constructed and arranged that neither of such brakes can be used without bringing into action simultaneously the brake attached to the vehicle drawn, or if the brake of the vehicle drawn can be applied from the light locomotive independently of the brakes of the latter

Article IV.—Every person driving or in charge of a light locomotive when used on any highway shall comply with the Regulations hereinafter set forth namely—

    (1) He shall not drive the light locomotive at any speed greater than is reasonable and proper having regard to the traffic on the highway, so as to endanger the life or limb of any person, or to the common danger of passengers

    (2) He shall not under any circumstances drive the light locomotive at a greater speed than twelve miles an hour If

the weight unladen of the light locomotive is one ton and a half and does not exceed two tons, he shall not drive the same at a greater speed than eight miles an hour, or if such weight exceeds two tons at a greater speed than five miles an hour

Provided that whatever may be the weight of the light locomotive, if it is used on any highway to draw any vehicle, he shall not under any circumstances drive it at a greater speed than six miles an hour

Provided also that this Regulation shall only have effect during six months from the date of this Order, and thereafter until We otherwise direct.

(3) He shall not cause the light locomotive to travel backwards for a greater distance or time than may be requisite for purposes of safety.

(4) He shall not negligently or wilfully cause any hurt or damage to any person, carriage, horse, or cattle, or to any goods conveyed in any carriage on any highway, or when on the light locomotive be in such a position that he cannot have control over the same, or quit the light locomotive without having taken due precautions against its being started in his absence, or allow the light locomotive or a vehicle drawn thereby to stand on such highway so as to cause any unnecessary obstruction thereof

(5) He shall when meeting any carriage, horse, or cattle keep the light locomotive on the left or near side of the road, and when passing any carriage, horse, or cattle proceeding in the same direction keep the light locomotive on the right or off side of the same

(6) He shall not negligently or wilfully prevent, hinder, or interrupt the free passage of any person, carriage, horse, or cattle on any highway, and shall keep the light locomotive and any vehicle drawn thereby on the left or near side of the road for the purpose of allowing such passage

(7) He shall, whenever necessary, by sounding the bell or other instrument required by Section 3 of the Act, give audible and sufficient warning of the approach or position of the light locomotive

(8) He shall on the request of any police constable, or of any person having charge of a restive horse, or on any such constable or person putting up his hand as a signal for that purpose, cause the light locomotive to stop and to remain stationary so long as may be reasonably necessary

Article V.—If the light locomotive is one to which Regulation 6 of Article II applies, and the particulars required by that Regulation are not duly painted thereon, or if the light locomotive is one to which that Regulation does not apply, the person driving or in charge thereof shall, on the request of any constable, or on the reasonable request of any other person, truly state his name and place of abode, and the name of the owner, and the place of his abode or business

This Order may be cited as "The Light Locomotives on Highways Order, 1896"

Light Locomotive to be deemed a Carriage

By Section 1 of the above-mentioned Act, a light locomotive is to be deemed to be a carriage within the meaning of any Act of Parliament, whether public, general, or local, and of any rule, regulation, or bye law made under any Act of Parliament, and if used as a carriage of any particular class, is to be deemed to be a carriage of that class, and the law relating to carriages of that class is to apply accordingly Consequently, if e g a light locomotive is used as a hackney or stage carriage, all statutory provisions and orders with regard to hackney and stage carriages in force in the Metropolitan Police District will apply thereto, and in addition the whole of the various statutes relating to highways which deal with the regulation of vehicular traffic apply equally

Driving to the Common Danger of Passengers

Attention is specially directed to Article 4, Regulations 1 and 2, as to the speed at which light locomotives may be driven, and it is to be clearly understood that any person using such carriage is not necessarily entitled to drive at the maximum rate of speed laid down in the Regulations, but only at such a rate as is reasonable and proper having regard to the traffic on the highway. The police will strictly enforce this Regulation in the Metropolis, and it is also to be noted that The Metropolitan Police Act, 1839, applies to the use of light locomotives, and provides that any person driving any such carriage to the common danger of passengers in any thoroughfare may be apprehended without warrant, and charged before a magistrate.

Any breach of the foregoing Regulations may, on conviction, be punished by a fine not exceeding Ten Pounds.

E. R. C. BRADFORD,

The Commissioner of Police of the Metropolis

METROPOLITAN POLICE OFFICE,
    NEW SCOTLAND YARD, S W

[*Undated*]

APPENDIX E.

COPY OF MR. ASQUITH'S AWARD.

The following scale is to be in force —

June	4 — July	15	6 weeks	at	16s.	per day.
July	16 — ,,	22	1 ,,	,,	15s.	,,
,,	23 — ,,	29	1 ,,	,,	14s	,,
,,	30 — August	5	1 ,,	,,	13s.	,,
August	6 — ,,	12	1 ,,	,,	12s	,,
,,	13 — ,,	19	1 ,,	,,	11s	,,
,,	20 — October	21	9 ,,	,,	10s.	,,
October	22 — ,,	28	1 ,,	,,	11s.	,,
,,	29 — January	14	11 ,,	,,	12s	,,
January	15 — April	1	11 ,,	,,	11s	,,
April	2 — ,,	15	2 ,,	,,	12s	,,
,,	16 — May	6	3 ,,	,,	13s	,,
May	7 — ,,	20	2 ,,	,,	14s	,,
,,	21 — June	3	2 ,,	,,	15s.	,,

The above scale is to regulate the net cash price to be paid per day by driver to owner for first-class street hansom cabs from this date. It is to be subject to revision as from the first Monday in April, 1895, if within fourteen days prior to that date notice demanding revision is given to me by or on behalf of either of the parties to the agreement of this day

(Signed) H H ASQUITH

11th June, 1894

MR ASQUITH'S AWARD

Having considered the statements made to me by representatives of proprietors and drivers respectively in reference to the price to be paid for four-wheeled cabs, I now fix the following scale :—

(1) The net cash price to be paid by driver to owner for best street iron-tyred four-wheeled cabs, with two horses per day, to be according to the subjoined scale —

May	14 — July	22	10 weeks at	13s.	per day
July	23 — August	12	3 ,,	12s	,,
August	13 — September	9	4 ,,	11s	,,
September	10 — March	26	28 ,,	10s	,,
March	27 — April	9	2 ,,	11s	,,
April	10 — May	14	5 ,,	12s	,,

(2) The net cash price to be paid by driver to owner for rubber-tyred four-wheeled cabs to be in all cases 1s. (one shilling) over the price for iron-tyred four-wheeled cabs.

(3) The net cash price to be paid by driver to owner for four wheeled cabs worked on the one-horse principle to be according to the subjoined scale —

June 4 — July 29	8 weeks at	8s.	per day
July 30 — April 2	35 ,,	6s 6d	,,
April 3 — May 7 .	5 ,,	7s.	,,
May 8 — June 3	4 ,,	7s. 6d	,,

(4) The actual amount charged by the Railway Companies for privileged cabs to be paid by the drivers to the owners in addition to the above

(Signed) H H ASQUITH

27th June, 1894.

THE LONDON HACKNEY CARRIAGE ACT, 1831.

(1-2 W IV 22)

An Act to Amend the Laws relating to Hackney Carriages and to Waggons, Carts, and Drays used in the Metropolis .   .

[22nd September, 1831.

1 to 3. *Repealed*

Definition of hackney carriage
4. Every carriage with two or more wheels which shall be used for the purpose of standing or plying for hire in any public street or road at any place within the distance of five miles from the General Post Office in the City of London, whatever may be the form or construction of such carriage, or the number of persons which the same shall be calculated to convey, or the number of horses by which the same shall be drawn, shall be deemed and taken to be a hackney carriage within the meaning of this Act, and in all proceedings at law or otherwise, and upon all occasions whatsoever, it shall be sufficient to describe any such carriage as aforesaid by the term "hackney carriage," without further or otherwise describing the same Provided always that nothing in this Act contained shall extend to any stage coach used for the purpose of standing or plying for passengers to be carried for hire at separate fares, and being duly licensed by the Commissioners of Stamps for that purpose, and having thereon the proper numbered plates required by law to be placed on such stage coaches

5 to 17. *Repealed*

Carriages, horses, harness, &c liable to duties and penalties.
18. All carriages, horses, and harness, and other articles and things, kept, used, or employed for the purpose of being let for hire by any person to whom any such licence as aforesaid shall be granted under the provisions of this Act, shall be subject and liable to and chargeable with all the duties which shall from time to time become due and

payable from or by such person for or in respect of any such licence as aforesaid granted to him, and to and with all penalties which may be imposed upon or incurred by such person under this Act, and also to and with the costs and expenses of all proceedings which shall or may be had or taken for the recovery of any such duties and penalties respectively, and all such carriages, horses, harness, and other articles and things may be distrained or otherwise seized or taken to satisfy such duties, penalties, costs, and expenses, or any part thereof respectively, in or into whose custody or possession soever such carriages, horses, harness, and other articles shall or may be or come, and by or under what right or title soever the same shall or may be held or claimed, and in case any person in or into whose custody or possession any such carriages, horses, harness, or other articles shall be or come, by or under any means or title whatsoever, shall convert the same to his own use, or shall sell or dispose thereof for the use or benefit of any other person, after notice given by the Commissioners of Stamps, or their solicitor, or by any other officer of stamp duties, that such carriages, horses, harness, or other articles are subject and liable to or chargeable with any of the duties, penalties, costs, and expenses aforesaid, every person so converting or selling or disposing of such carriages, horses, harness, or other articles shall be accountable to His Majesty to the extent of the value of such carriages, horses, harness, or other articles, for the duties, penalties, costs, and expenses to or with which such carriages, horses, harness, or other articles shall be subject, liable, or chargeable, and the same may be sued for and recovered under and by virtue of this Act as a debt due to His Majesty accordingly

19 to 26. *Repealed*

27. All pecuniary penalties and costs incurred by reason of any offence committed by the driver of any hackney carriage against the provisions of this Act shall, unless such driver shall pay the same, be levied by distress and sale of the goods of the proprietor of such hackney carriage, and for want of sufficient distress such proprietor shall be committed to the common gaol or house of correction *Penalties if not paid by drivers to be levied on proprietors*

28. Provided always that every such proprietor who shall pay any penalty or costs incurred by reason of any such offence as aforesaid committed by such driver shall be entitled to recover the same from such driver in a summary *Who shall be entitled to recover from the drivers*

manner, and upon complaint made in the premises before any justice of the peace by the said proprietor against the said driver, such justice shall inquire into the same, and shall cause the sum which shall appear to have been so paid as aforesaid by the said proprietor to be levied by distress and sale of the goods of the said driver, and for want of sufficient distress such justice shall commit the said driver to the common gaol or house of correction, there to remain for any time not exceeding two calendar months, unless the said sum shall be sooner paid; and every such imprisonment shall be with or without hard labour, as such justice shall direct. Provided always that if the said driver shall have been previously convicted of the offence for which the said penalty or costs shall be so as aforesaid paid by the said proprietor, then such proceedings shall be had and taken against the said driver upon such conviction for recovery of the penalty and costs in which he shall have been convicted as might have been had and taken thereon in case the said penalty or costs had not been paid by the said proprietor, and upon recovery thereof the sum so paid by such proprietor shall be repaid to him

29 to 34. *Repealed*

Hackney carriages standing in any street to be deemed to be plying for hire, and the driver thereof refusing to go with any person liable to a penalty of 40s.

35. Every hackney carriage which shall be found standing in any street or place, and having thereon any of the numbered plates required by this Act to be fixed on hackney carriages, shall, unless actually hired, be deemed to be plying for hire, although such hackney carriage shall not be on any standing or place usually appropriated for the purpose of hackney carriages standing or plying for hire, and the driver of every such hackney carriage which shall not be actually hired shall be obliged and compellable to go with any person desirous of hiring such hackney carriage, and upon the hearing of any complaint against the driver of any such hackney carriage for any such refusal, such driver shall be obliged to adduce evidence of having been and of being actually hired at the time of such refusal, and in case such driver shall fail to produce sufficient evidence of having been and of being so hired as aforesaid, he shall forfeit forty shillings

Compensation to be made to drivers improperly summoned

36. Provided always that if the driver of any hackney carriage shall in civil and explicit terms declare to any person desirous to hire such hackney carriage that it is actually hired, and shall afterwards, notwithstanding such reply, be summoned to answer for his refusal to carry such person in his said hackney carriage, and shall upon the hearing of the complaint produce sufficient evidence to prove that such hackney carriage was at the time actually and *bonâ fide* hired, and it shall not appear that he used uncivil language, or that he improperly conducted himself towards the party by whom he shall be so summoned, the justice before whom such complaint shall be heard shall order the person who shall have summoned such driver to make to him such compensation for his loss of time in attending to make his defence to such complaint as such justice shall deem reasonable, and in default of payment thereof to commit such person to prison for any time not exceeding one calendar month, unless the same shall be sooner paid *[for refusing to carry any person.]*

37. It shall be lawful for the proprietor or driver of any hackney carriage which shall be licensed under the authority of this Act to stand and ply for hire with such carriage and to drive the same on the Lord's Day, any former Act or Acts to the contrary notwithstanding, and that such proprietor or driver who shall so stand or ply for hire as aforesaid shall be liable and compellable to do the like work on the Lord's Day as such proprietor or driver is by this Act liable or compellable to do on any other day of the week *[Drivers may ply and shall be compellable to drive on Sundays]*

38 to 40. *Repealed.*

41. If any person shall refuse or omit to pay the driver of any hackney carriage the sum justly due to him for the hire of such hackney carriage, or if any person shall deface or in any manner injure any such hackney carriage, it shall be lawful for any justice of the peace, upon complaint thereof made to him, to grant a summons, or if it shall appear to him necessary, a warrant, for bringing before him or any other justice such defaulter or defender [sic], and, upon proof of the facts made upon oath before any such justice, to award reasonable satisfaction to the party so complaining for his fare or for his damages and costs, and also reasonable compensation for his loss of time in attending to make and establish such complaint, and upon the refusal of such defaulter or offender to pay or make such satisfaction it shall be lawful for such justice to commit him to prison, there to remain for any time not exceeding one calendar month, unless the amount of such satisfaction shall be sooner paid, and it shall also be lawful for such justice, if he shall think fit, to order such defaulter or offender to be kept to hard labour during such imprisonment *[Persons refusing to pay the driver his fare, or for any damage, may be committed to prison]*

42. *Repealed*

Agreement to pay more than the legal fare not to be binding.

Sum paid beyond the proper fare may be recovered back

Penalty 40s.

43. No agreement whatever made with the driver of any hackney carriage for the payment of more than his proper fare, as the same is allowed and limited by this Act, shall be binding on the person making the same, but any such person may, notwithstanding any such agreement, refuse, on discharging such hackney carriage, the payment of any sum beyond the proper fare as allowed and limited as aforesaid; and in case any person shall actually pay to the driver of any hackney carriage, whether in pursuance of any such agreement or not, any sum exceeding his said proper fare, which shall have been demanded or required by such driver, the person paying the same shall be entitled, on complaint made against such driver before any justice of the peace, to recover back the sum paid beyond the proper fare, and moreover such driver shall forfeit, as a penalty for such exaction, the sum of forty shillings; and in default of the repayment by such driver of such excess of fare, or of payment of the said penalty, such justice shall forthwith commit such driver to prison, there to remain for any time not exceeding one calendar month, unless the said excess of fare and the said penalty shall be sooner paid

Driver not to charge more than the sum agreed for, although the distance be exceeded

Penalty 40s.

44. It shall be lawful for any person to require the driver of any hackney carriage to drive such hackney carriage for a stated sum of money, a distance in the discretion of such driver, and in case such driver shall exceed the distance to which such person was entitled to be driven for such stated sum of money, such driver shall not exact or demand more than the sum for which he was so engaged to drive, upon pain to forfeit forty shillings for such offence

Penalty for demanding more than the sum agreed for, though less than the legal fare, 40s

45. If the proprietor or driver of any hackney carriage, or if any other person on his behalf and with his knowledge and consent, shall agree beforehand with any person hiring such hackney carriage to take for any job any sum less than the proper rate of fare allowed by this Act, such proprietor or driver shall not exact or demand for his fare more than the sum agreed for, upon pain to forfeit forty shillings for such offence

46. *Repealed*

Deposit to be made for carriages waiting

47. Where any hackney carriage shall be hired and taken to any place of public resort, or elsewhere, and the driver thereof shall be required there to wait with such hackney carriage, it shall be lawful for such driver to demand and receive from the person so hiring and requiring him to wait as aforesaid a reasonable sum as a deposit, over and above the fare to which such driver shall be entitled for driving thither, which sum so demanded and received shall be accounted for by such driver when such hackney carriage shall be finally discharged; and if any such driver who shall have received any such deposit as aforesaid shall refuse to wait with such hackney carriage at the place where he shall be so required to wait, or if such driver shall go away, or shall permit such hackney carriage to be driven or taken away, without the consent of the person making such deposit, before the expiration of the time for which the sum so deposited shall be a sufficient compensation; or if such driver on the final discharge of such hackney carriage shall refuse duly to account for such deposit, every such driver so offending shall forfeit forty shillings. *Penalty on the driver refusing to wait, or to account for the deposit, 40s.*

48. The proprietor of every hackney carriage shall provide and place in such hackney carriage a proper check string or wire, and shall renew the same from time to time so often as occasion shall require; and the driver of every such hackney carriage shall, during the time of his driving any person in such hackney carriage, hold such check string or wire in his hand, so that the same may be used for the accommodation of such person; and if the proprietor of any such hackney carriage shall neglect to provide and place in such hackney carriage such check string or wire as aforesaid, or shall neglect to renew the same when and so often as shall be requisite, or if the driver of any such hackney carriage shall neglect or refuse to hold such check string or wire in his hand during the time aforesaid, every such proprietor and every such driver so offending respectively shall forfeit twenty shillings. *Proprietors to provide check strings, drivers to hold same in their hands. Penalty 20s.*

49. *Repealed*

50. If the proprietor or driver of any hackney carriage which shall be hired shall permit or suffer any person to ride or be carried in, upon, or about such hackney carriage, without the express consent of the person hiring the same, such proprietor or driver shall forfeit twenty shillings. *Penalty for permitting persons to ride without consent of the hirer, 20s.*

51. If any proprietor or driver of any hackney carriage shall stand or ply for hire with such hackney carriage, or suffer the same to stand, across any street or common *Improperly standing with carriage, or* *feeding horses in the street.*

passage or alley, or alongside of any other hackney carriage, or two in a breadth, or within eight feet of the curbstone of the pavement in any such street or common passage or alley; or if any such proprietor or driver . . or other person shall feed the horses of or belonging to any hackney carriage in any street, road, or common passage, save only with corn out of a bag, or with hay which he shall hold or deliver with his hands; or if the driver of any hackney carriage shall refuse to give way if he conveniently can to any private coach or other carriage, or shall obstruct or hinder the driver of any other hackney carriage in taking up or setting down any person into or from such other hackney carriage; or if any such proprietor or driver shall wrongfully, in a forcible or clandestine manner, take away the fare from any other such proprietor or driver who, in the judgment of any justice of the peace before whom any complaint of such offence shall be heard, shall appear to be fairly entitled to such fare, every such proprietor, driver . . or other person so offending shall forfeit twenty shillings

Refusing to give way to or obstructing any other driver, or depriving him of his fare

Penalty 20s.

52 to 54. *Repealed.*

Penalty for leaving carriages unattended at places of public resort, 20s.

55. If the driver of any hackney carriage shall leave such hackney carriage unattended in any street or road, or at any place of public resort or entertainment, whether such carriage shall be hired or not, it shall be lawful for any officer of police, constable, or other peace officer, watchman, or patrole, to drive away such hackney carriage, and to deposit the same, with the horse or horses belonging or harnessed thereto, at some neighbouring livery stables or other place of safe custody, and such driver shall forfeit twenty shillings for such offence; and in default of payment of the said penalty upon conviction, and of the expenses of taking and keeping the said hackney carriage or horse or horses, the same, together with the harness belonging thereto, or any of them, shall be sold by order of the justice before whom such conviction shall be made, and after deducting from the produce of such sale the amount of the said penalty, and of all costs and expenses as well of the proceedings before such justice as of the taking, keeping, and sale of the sale of the said hackney carriage, and of the said horse or horses and harness, the surplus (if any) of the said produce shall be paid to the proprietor of such hackney carriage

Proprietors, drivers . . . . misbehaving.

56. If the proprietor or driver of any hackney carriage, or any other person having the care thereof, shall, by intoxication, or by wanton and furious driving, or by any

other wilful misconduct, injure or endanger any person in his life, limbs, or property, or if any such proprietor or driver .. shall make use of any abusive or insulting language, or be guilty of other rude behaviour, to or towards any person whatever, or shall assault or obstruct any officer of stamp duties or any officer of police, constable or other peace officer, watchman, or patrole, in the execution of his duty, every such proprietor, driver . or other person so offending in any of the several cases aforesaid, shall forfeit five pounds, and in default of payment thereof he shall be committed to the common gaol or house of correction and after the conviction of any such proprietor .. for any such offence as aforesaid, it shall be lawful for the Commissioners of Stamps, if they shall think fit, to revoke the licence of any such proprietor .... and to refuse to grant him any further licence in future Penalty £5.
Licence may be revoked.

57. If any driver of a hackney carriage . shall be summoned or brought before any justice of the peace to answer any complaint or information touching or concerning any offence committed or alleged to have been committed by such driver . against the provisions of this Act, and such complaint or information shall afterwards be withdrawn or quashed or dismissed, or if the defendant shall be acquitted of the offence charged against him, it shall be lawful for the said justice, if he shall think fit, to order and award that the complainant or informant shall pay to the said driver . such compensation for his loss of time in attending the said justice touching or concerning such complaint or information as to the said justice shall seem reasonable, and in default of payment of such compensation it shall be lawful for the said justice to commit such complainant or informant to prison for any time not exceeding one calendar month, unless the same shall be sooner paid Justices empowered to award compensation to drivers for their loss of time in attending to answer complaints which shall not be substantiated against them

58. *Repealed*

59. The owner of every waggon, wain, cart, car, dray, or other such carriage which shall be driven or used in any public street or road within the distance of five miles from the General Post Office in the City of London, shall, before such waggon, wain, cart, car, dray, or other such carriage shall be so driven or used as aforesaid, paint or cause to be painted in words at full length, and in one or more straight line or lines, upon some conspicuous place on the right or off side of such waggon, wain, cart, car, dray, or Names and places of abode of owners of waggons, carts, &c., to be painted thereon

other such carriage, clear of the wheel or wheels thereof, or upon the right or off side shaft thereof, the true Christian name and surname and place of abode of the owner or (if there be more than one) of the principal owner of such waggon, wain, cart, car, dray, or other such carriage, and the letters of all such words shall be painted in legible and conspicuous characters of black upon a white ground or of white upon a black ground, and shall be at least one inch in height and of proper and proportionate breadth, and all such words shall be repainted or renewed in like manner from time to time as often as the same or any part thereof shall become obliterated or defaced

<small>Penalty for using waggons &c upon which the names and places of abode are not painted, £5.</small>

60. If any person shall drive or use, or cause to be driven or used, in or upon any public street or road within the distance of five miles from the said General Post Office, any waggon, wain, cart, car, dray, or other such carriage upon which there shall not be duly painted in such legible and conspicuous characters as aforesaid, and in the manner directed by this Act, the true Christian name and surname and place of abode of the owner or (if there be more than one) of the principal owner of such waggon, wain, cart, car, dray, or other such carriage, every person so offending shall forfeit five pounds, and it shall be lawful for any person to take and seize such waggon, wain, cart, car, dray, or other such carriage, and any horse drawing the same, and to lodge the same for safe custody at some public green yard or some livery stables or other place of safety, and them to detain and keep until some one of His Majesty's justices of the peace shall hear and determine such offence, and until the penalty which such offender shall be liable and adjudged to pay for such offence, together with the costs of the proceedings for the recovery thereof, and the expenses of taking and keeping such waggon, wain, cart, car, dray, or other carriage, and any horse drawing the same, shall be fully paid and discharged, and if, on the conviction of any such offender, the said penalty, costs, and expenses shall not be forthwith paid, such waggon, wain, cart, car, dray, or other such carriage, and the horse, so seized and taken as aforesaid, or either of them, shall be sold, under an order for that purpose under the hand of such justice, directed to the constable or other peace officer of the parish or place where any such offence shall be committed, and the surplus (if any) of the money arising from such sale, after deducting thereout the amount of such penalty, costs, and expenses as aforesaid, together also with the costs and expenses of such sale, shall be rendered to the owner of the waggon, wain, cart, car, dray, or other carriage or horse which shall have been so seized and sold as aforesaid

61. *Repealed*

62. It shall be lawful for His Majesty's Principal Secretary of State for the Home Department, by such orders and under such regulations as he shall from time to time think fit to make in that behalf, to direct any one of His Majesty's justices of the peace, appointed or to be appointed under any Act or Acts for regulating the office of a justice of peace in the Metropolis, to attend daily from the hour of eleven in the forenoon until the hour of three in the afternoon at such one of the public police offices of the Metropolis, or at such other office or place as the said Principal Secretary of State shall appoint in that behalf, not being within the City of London, for the purpose of hearing and determining offences against the provisions of this Act, and that it shall be lawful for any justice of the peace who for the time being shall be in attendance at such public police office, or other office or place to be appointed for that purpose as aforesaid, to hear and determine all such offences as aforesaid in a summary manner, wheresoever the same may have been committed Provided always that it shall also be lawful for any other of His Majesty's justices of the peace, having jurisdiction where any such offence as aforesaid shall be committed, in like manner to hear and determine the same at any place within his jurisdiction.

Before whom offences shall be heard and determined.

63. It shall be lawful for any such justice as aforesaid, in all cases in which no other mode of proceeding is specially provided or directed by this Act, upon information or complaint made by any person of any offence against the provisions of this Act, within thirty days next after the commission of any such offence, to summon the party accused, and also the witnesses on either side, to appear before the said justice, or before any other justice of the peace, at a time and place to be appointed for that purpose, and either on the appearance of the party accused, or in default thereof, it shall be lawful for such justice, or any other justice present at the time and place appointed for such appearance, to proceed to examine into the matter of fact, and upon due proof made thereof by voluntary confession of the party, or by oath of one or more credible witness or witnesses, to give judgment for the penalty or forfeiture, and on nonpayment thereof, together with the

Mode of proceeding for penalties before a justice of the peace

costs of such proceedings, to commit the offender to prison where such commitment is specially directed by this Act; and in any case where such commitment is not so specially directed such justice is hereby required to award and issue out of [*sic*] his warrant for the levying of any penalty or forfeiture so adjudged, together with the said costs and expenses, and also the costs and expenses of such warrant, and of levying the same on the goods of the offender, and to cause sale to be made of such goods in case they shall not be redeemed within five days, rendering to the party the overplus (if any), and where goods of such offender cannot be found sufficient to answer the penalty, and all such costs and expenses, to commit such offender to prison, there to remain for any time not exceeding two calendar months unless such penalty and all such costs and expenses shall be sooner paid, and every such imprisonment shall be with or without hard labour, as such justice shall direct

64 to 67. *Repealed.*

Service of justice's summons

68. Any summons issued by any justice of the peace requiring the appearance of any defendant or of any witness or other person, with reference to any information, complaint, or other proceeding pending for the recovery of any duty or penalty under this Act, shall be deemed to be well and sufficiently served in case either the summons or a copy thereof be served personally on any such person as aforesaid, or be left at his usual or last place of abode, or (in case such person be a licensed proprietor of a hackney carriage) at the place specified in any such licence as the place of abode of such proprietor and if the place so specified cannot be found, or if such proprietor shall not be known thereat, then such summons shall be deemed to be well and sufficiently served if the same or a copy thereof be fixed up in some conspicuous place in the said head office for stamps to be appointed for that purpose

69. *Repealed*

Justices may mitigate penalties.

70. It shall be lawful for any justice of the peace before whom any person shall be convicted of any offence against any of the provisions of this Act to mitigate, as he shall think fit, any penalty by this Act imposed, in cases where such justice shall see cause so to do

71. All pecuniary penalties which shall be recovered before any justice of the peace under the provisions of this Act, except such as shall be recovered in the City of London or the Borough of Southwark, shall respectively be divided and distributed in manner following that is to say—one moiety thereof to His Majesty, and the other moiety thereof (with full costs) to the person who shall inform and prosecute for the same *[Distribution of penalties.]*

72 and 73. *Repealed*

74. Whenever in this Act, with reference to any person, animal, matter or thing, any word or words is or are used importing the singular number or the masculine gender only, yet such word or words shall be understood to include several persons or animals as well as one person or animal, females as well as males, bodies politic or corporate as well as individuals, and several matters or things as well as one matter or thing, unless it be otherwise specially provided, or there be something in the subject or context repugnant to such construction. *[Construction of the terms used in this Act]*

75 to 78. *Repealed*

Schedules. *Repealed.*

THE LONDON HACKNEY CARRIAGES ACT, 1843.

(6-7 V. 86).

An Act for regulating Hackney and Stage Carriages in and near London.
[22nd August, 1843

1. *Repealed*

Meaning of certain words used in this Act.

2. The words hereinafter mentioned, which in their usual signification have a more confined or different meaning, shall in this Act (except where the nature of the provisions or the context of the Act shall exclude such construction) be interpreted as follows (that is to say) the words "hackney carriage" shall include every carriage (except a stage carriage) which shall stand on hire or ply for a passenger for hire at any place within the limits of the City of London and the liberties thereof and Metropolitan Police District, and the words "metropolitan stage carriage" shall include every stage carriage, except such as shall on every journey go to or come from some town or place beyond the limits aforesaid, and the word "proprietor" shall include every person who, either alone or in partnership with any other person, shall keep any hackney carriage or any metropolitan stage carriage, or who shall be concerned otherwise than as a driver or attendant in employing for hire any hackney carriage or any metropolitan stage carriage, and the word "conductor" shall include every director or other person, except the driver, who shall attend upon the passengers in any metropolitan stage carriage . . and the word "passenger" shall include every person carried by any hackney carriage, or by any metropolitan stage carriage, except one driver, and, where there shall be a conductor to such metropolitan stage carriage, one conductor, and the word "horse" shall include every mare and gelding, and every word importing the singular number only shall extend and be applied to several persons and things as well as to one person or thing; and every word importing the masculine gender only shall extend to a female as well as to a male

3. So much of an Act passed in the second year of the reign of His late Majesty, intituled "An Act to Amend the Laws relating to Hackney Carriages, and to Waggons, Carts, and Drays used in the Metropolis; and to Place the Collection of the Duties on Hackney Carriages and on Hawkers and Pedlars in England under the Commissioners of Stamps," as relates to hackney carriages ... and not hereby repealed   shall extend and apply to hackney carriages   . within the meaning of this Act . {Certain provisions of 1 & 2 Will IV. c 22 extended to this Act.}

4. And whereas by the said recited Act passed in the reign of His late Majesty it was enacted that the owner of every waggon, cart, car, dray, or other carriage should, before any such carriage should be driven or used in any public street or road, within the distance of five miles from the General Post Office in the City of London, paint or cause to be painted in words at full length, and in one or more straight line or lines, upon some conspicuous place on the right or off side of every such carriage, clear of the wheel or wheels thereof, or upon the right or off-side shaft thereof, the true Christian name and surname and place of abode of the owner, or, if there be more than one, of the principal owner of such carriage, in the manner in such Act directed · Be it enacted that in all cases where the owner of any such carriage shall be a peer of the realm, or shall be known or usually designated by some title of rank, it shall be deemed to be a compliance with the provisions of the aforesaid Act that the title only and place of abode of such peer or other person shall be painted in the manner therein described upon any such waggon, wain, cart, or other carriage. {Title and place of abode of a peer of the realm painted on any carriage &c to be deemed a compliance with the provisions of the Act.}

5 and 6. *Repealed*

7. The proprietor of every metropolitan stage carriage shall keep distinctly painted, both on the outside and inside of the same, in such a manner and in such a position as shall from time to time be directed by the registrar, the words "Metropolitan Stage Carriage," or such other words as the registrar shall direct   . and shall also, on the inside of every such carriage, keep distinctly painted in a conspicuous manner a table of fares to be demanded of passengers by such carriage, and the fares therein specified {Particulars to be painted on metropolitan stage carriages}

shall be deemed to be the only lawful fares, and may be recovered by the driver or conductor as in the case of hackney carriages, in a summary way, before any justice of the peace, and every proprietor making default in the premises shall forfeit the sum of twenty shillings for every offence

Registrar to grant licences.

8. It shall be lawful for the registrar to grant a licence to act as driver of hackney carriages, or as driver or as conductor of metropolitan stage carriages .. (as the case may be) to any person who shall produce such a certificate as shall satisfy the said registrar of his good behaviour and fitness for such situation respectively Provided always that no person shall be licensed as such driver as aforesaid who is under sixteen years of age; and in every such licence shall be specified the number of such licence, and the proper name and surname, and place of abode, and age, and a description of the person to whom such licence shall be granted and every such licence shall bear date on the day on which the same shall be granted .. . and on every licence of a driver or conductor the registrar shall cause proper columns to be prepared, in which every proprietor employing the driver or conductor named in such licence shall enter his own name and address and the day on which such driver or conductor shall enter into and shall quit his service respectively, and in case any of the particulars entered or endorsed upon any licence in pursuance of this Act shall be erased or defaced every such licence shall be wholly void and of none effect; and the said registrar shall,

At the time of granting any licence an abstract of the laws and a ticket to be given.

at the time of granting any licence, deliver to the driver or conductor . to whom the same shall be granted an abstract of the laws in force relating to such driver or conductor and of the penalties to which he is liable for any misconduct, and also a metal ticket, upon which there shall be marked or engraved his office or employment, and a number corresponding with the number which shall be inserted in such licence

9. *Repealed.*

Penalty on persons acting as drivers &c. without licences and tickets, £5.

10. It shall not be lawful for any person to act as driver of any hackney carriage, or as driver or conductor of any metropolitan stage carriage, whether such person shall or shall not be the proprietor of such carriage within the limits of this Act, unless in each case such person shall have a licence so to do, and a numbered ticket granted to him under the authority of this Act, and remaining in

force, and every person who shall act as such driver or conductor without such licence and ticket .. and also every person to whom a licence and ticket shall have been granted, who shall, except in compliance with the provisions of this Act, transfer or lend such licence, or permit any other person to use or wear such ticket, shall for every such offence forfeit the sum of five pounds, and every proprietor who shall knowingly suffer any person not duly licensed under the authority of this Act to act as driver of any hackney carriage, or as driver or as conductor of any metropolitan stage carriage, of which he shall be the proprietor, shall for every such offence forfeit the sum of ten pounds Provided always that nothing hereinbefore contained shall subject to any penalty any proprietor who shall employ any unlicensed person to act as such driver or conductor as aforesaid for any time not exceeding twenty-four hours, or any unlicensed person who shall be so employed for the said time, upon proof being adduced by the proprietor to the satisfaction of the justice of the peace before whom such proprietor, driver, or conductor shall be required to attend to answer for such offences respectively, that such employment was occasioned by unavoidable necessity, and that every proprietor who shall so employ such unlicensed driver or conductor, and every such unlicensed driver or conductor, shall be subject to all the powers, provisions, and proceedings of and under this Act or the said recited Act of His late Majesty for any Act done by such driver or conductor during such employment, in like manner as if such driver or conductor had been duly licensed

On proprietors suffering drivers or conductors so to do, £10.

11 to 13. *Repealed*

14. Before any such licence as aforesaid shall be granted a requisition for the same, in such form as the said registrar shall from time to time appoint for that purpose, and accompanied with such certificate as hereinbefore is required, shall be made and signed by the person by whom such licence shall be required, and in every such requisition all such particulars as the registrar shall require shall be truly set forth, and every person applying for or attempting to procure any such licence who shall make or cause to be made any false representation in regard to any of the said particulars, or who shall endeavour to obtain a licence by any forged recommendations, or who shall not truly answer all questions which shall be demanded of him in

Persons applying for licences to sign a requisition for the same

relation to such application for a licence, and also every person to whom reference shall be made who shall, in regard to such application, wilfully and knowingly make any misrepresentation, shall forfeit for every such offence the sum of five pounds; and it shall be lawful for the registrar to proceed for recovering of such penalty before any magistrate at any time within one calendar month after the commission of the offence, or during the currency of the licence so improperly obtained

Notice to be given by drivers, conductors, of any change of abode.

15. As often as any driver or conductor ... shall change his place of abode he shall give notice thereof in writing, signed by him, to the said registrar, specifying in such notice his new place of abode, and shall at the same time produce his licence to the said registrar, who shall endorse thereon a memorandum specifying the particulars of such change, and every driver, conductor, who shall change his place of abode, and shall neglect for two days to give notice of such change, and to produce his licence in order that such memorandum as aforesaid may be endorsed thereon, shall forfeit for every such offence the sum of twenty shillings, and it shall be lawful for the registrar, or for any person employed by him for that purpose, to sue for such penalty at any time during the currency of such licence

Particulars of licences to be entered in a book at the registrar's office.

16. The particulars of every licence which shall be granted as aforesaid shall be entered in books to be kept for that purpose at the office of the said registrar, and in all courts, and before any justice of the peace, and upon all occasions whatsoever, a copy of any entry made in any such book, and certified by the person having the charge thereof to be a true copy, shall be received as evidence, and be deemed sufficient proof of all things therein registered, without requiring the production of the said book, or of any licence, or of any requisition or other document upon which any such entry may be founded, and every person applying at all reasonable times shall be furnished with a certified copy of the particulars respecting any licensed person without payment of any fee

Tickets to be worn by drivers

17. Every licensed driver and conductor . shall at all times during his employment, and when he shall be required to attend before any justice of the peace, wear his ticket conspicuously upon his breast, in such manner that the whole of the writing thereon shall be distinctly legible, and every driver or conductor ..
who shall act as such, or who shall attend when required

before any justice of the peace without wearing such ticket in manner aforesaid, or who, when thereunto required, shall refuse to produce such ticket for inspection, or to permit any person to note the writing thereon, shall for every such offence forfeit the sum of forty shillings

18. Upon the expiration of any licence granted under this Act the person to whom such licence shall have been granted shall deliver such licence and the ticket relating thereto to the said registrar, and every such person who, after the expiration of such licence, shall wilfully neglect for three days to deliver the same to the said registrar, and also every person who shall use or wear or detain any ticket, without having a licence in force relating to such ticket, or who shall for the purpose of deception use or wear or have any ticket resembling or intended to resemble any ticket granted under the authority of this Act, shall for every such offence forfeit the sum of five pounds, and it shall be lawful for the registrar, or for any person employed by him for that purpose, to prosecute any person so neglecting to deliver up his licence or ticket at any period within twelve calendar months after the expiration of the licence, and it shall be lawful for any constable or peace officer, or any person employed for that purpose by the registrar, to seize and take away any such ticket, wheresoever the same may be found, in order to deliver the same to the said registrar
Licences and tickets to be delivered up on the discontinuance of licences.

19. Whenever the writing on any ticket shall become obliterated or defaced, so that the same shall not be distinctly legible, and also whenever any ticket shall be proved to the satisfaction of the said registrar to have been lost or mislaid, the person to whom the licence relating to any such ticket shall have been granted shall deliver such ticket (if he shall have the same in his possession), and shall produce such licence to the said registrar, and such person shall then be entitled to have a new ticket delivered to him, upon payment, for the use of Her Majesty, of such sum of money, not exceeding three shillings, as the registrar shall from time to time appoint provided always that if any ticket which shall have been proved as aforesaid or represented to have been lost or mislaid, shall afterwards be found, the same shall forthwith be delivered to the said registrar, and every person into whose possession any such ticket as last aforesaid shall be or come who shall refuse or neglect for three days to deliver the same to the said registrar, and
New tickets to be delivered instead of defaced or lost tickets.

also every person licensed under the authority of this Act who shall use or wear the ticket granted to him after the writing thereon shall be obliterated, defaced, or obscured, so that the same shall not be distinctly legible, shall for every such offence forfeit the sum of forty shillings

<small>Forgery of licence or ticket or knowingly uttering a forged licence or ticket a misdemeanour</small>

20. Every person who shall forge or counterfeit, or who shall cause or procure to be forged or counterfeited, any licence or ticket by this Act directed to be provided for the driver of a hackney carriage, or for the driver or the conductor for a metropolitan stage carriage and also every person who shall sell or exchange, or expose to sale, or utter any such forged or counterfeited licence or ticket, and also every person who shall knowingly and without lawful excuse (the proof whereof shall lie on the person accused) have or be possessed of such forged or counterfeited licence or ticket, knowing such licence or ticket to be forged or counterfeited, and also every person knowingly and wilfully aiding and abetting any person in committing any such offence as aforesaid, shall be guilty of a misdemeanor, and being thereof convicted shall be liable to be punished by fine or imprisonment, or by both, such imprisonment to be in the common gaol or house of correction, and either with or without hard labour, as the Court shall think fit, and it shall be lawful for any person to detain any such licence or ticket or for any constable or peace officer, or any person employed for that purpose by the said registrar, to seize and take away any such licence or ticket, in order that the same may be produced in evidence against such offender, or be disposed of as the said registrar shall think proper.

<small>Proprietor to retain the licences of drivers or conductors employed by him, and produce them in case of complaint</small>

21. Every proprietor of a hackney carriage and of every metropolitan stage carriage who shall permit or employ any licensed person to act as the driver or conductor thereof shall require to be delivered to him, and shall retain in his possession, the licence of such driver or conductor while such driver or conductor shall remain in his service, and in all cases of complaint where the proprietor of a hackney carriage or of a metropolitan stage carriage shall be summoned to produce the driver or conductor of such carriage before a justice of the peace, he shall also produce the licence of such driver or conductor, if at the time of receiving the summons such driver or conductor shall be in his service, and if any driver or conductor complained of shall be adjudged guilty of the offence alleged against him, the justice of the peace before whom he shall be convicted shall in every case endorse upon the licence of such driver or conductor the nature of the offence, and the amount of the penalty inflicted, and every proprietor who shall neglect to require to be delivered to him, and to retain in his possession, the licence of any driver or conductor during such period as such driver or conductor shall remain in his service, or who shall refuse or neglect to produce such licence as aforesaid, shall for every such offence forfeit the sum of three pounds

22. It shall be lawful for any justice of the peace to hear and determine all matters of complaint between any proprietor of a hackney carriage or metropolitan stage carriage and the driver or conductor of the same respectively, and to order payment of any sum of money that shall appear to be due to either party for wages or for the earnings in respect of any such carriage, or on account of any deposit of money, and to order compensation to the proprietor in respect of damage or loss which shall have arisen through the neglect or default of any driver or conductor to the property of his employer entrusted to his care, or in respect of any sum of money which such proprietor may have been lawfully ordered by a justice of the peace to pay, and which has been actually paid pursuant to such order, on account of the negligence or wilful misconduct of his driver or conductor, and to order such compensation to either party in respect of any other matter of complaint between them as to such justice shall seem proper *Magistrates to hear and determine disputes.*

23. Provided always that it shall not be lawful, either in any Court of Law or before any justice of the peace, to enforce the payment of any sum of money claimed from any driver or conductor by any proprietor on account of the earnings of any hackney carriage or metropolitan stage carriage, unless under an agreement in writing, which shall have been signed by such driver or conductor in the presence of a competent witness, and no such agreement shall be liable to any stamp duty. *Agreements between drivers &c and proprietors to be in writing.*

24. When any licensed driver or conductor shall leave the service of any proprietor, such proprietor shall, upon demand thereof, return to him his licence provided always that if the said proprietor shall have any complaint against the said driver or conductor, it shall be lawful for such proprietor to retain the licence for any time not exceeding twenty-four hours after the demand thereof, and within that time to apply to the police court of the district in *Proceedings with respect to licences on quitting service.*

which the said proprietor shall dwell, or if he shall dwell in the City of London or the liberties thereof then to some justice of the said city, for a summons against him, and the said proprietor, at the time of applying for the summons, shall deposit the licence with the clerk of such police court or justice, and in case any proprietor who, upon demand thereof, shall have refused or neglected to deliver to any driver or conductor his licence shall not within twenty four hours, exclusive of Sunday or any day on which the police court shall not sit, apply for such summons and deposit the licence as aforesaid, or shall not appear to prosecute his complaint at the time mentioned in the summons, it shall be lawful for such driver or conductor to apply at the same police court, or to some justice as aforesaid, for a summons against such proprietor, and upon hearing and deciding the case the justice, if he shall think there was no just cause for detaining the licence, or that there has been needless delay on the part of the proprietor in bringing the matter to a hearing, shall have power to order the said proprietor to pay such compensation to the said driver or conductor as the said justice shall think reasonable, and payment of such compensation shall be enforced in the same manner as any penalty may be enforced under this Act by such justice, and the justice shall cause the licence to be delivered to the said driver or conductor, unless any misconduct shall be proved against him by reason whereof the justice shall think that such licence should be revoked or suspended, and so long as any proprietor shall neglect to apply for such summons and deposit the licence, after the demand thereof, any justice of the peace may in like manner from time to time order compensation to be paid by him to the same driver or conductor, and no proprietor shall, under any pretence or by virtue of any claim whatever, retain beyond the time aforesaid the licence of his driver or conductor

Licence may be revoked or suspended

25. It shall be lawful for any justice of the peace before whom any driver or conductor . . shall be convicted of any offence, whether under this Act or any other Act, if such justice shall in his discretion think fit, to revoke the licence of such driver or conductor and also any other licence which he shall hold under the provisions of this Act, or to suspend the same for such time as the justice shall think proper, and for that purpose to require the proprietor, driver, or conductor in whose possession such licence and the ticket thereunto belonging shall then be to deliver up the same, and every proprietor, driver, or conductor . .

who, being so required, shall refuse or neglect to deliver up such licence and any such ticket, or either or them, shall forfeit, so often as he shall be so required and refuse or neglect as aforesaid, the sum of five pounds, and the justice shall forthwith send such licence and ticket to the registrar, who shall cancel such licence if it has been revoked by the justice, or, if it has been suspended, shall, at the end of the time for which it shall have been suspended, re-deliver such licence, with the ticket, to the person to whom it was granted

26. *Repealed*

27. Every driver or conductor authorised by any proprietor to act as driver of any hackney carriage, or as driver or conductor of any metropolitan stage carriage, who shall suffer any other person to act as driver of such hackney carriage, or as driver or conductor of such metropolitan stage carriage, without the consent of the proprietor thereof, and also every person, whether duly licensed or not, who shall act as driver or conductor of any such carriage without the consent of the proprietor thereof, shall forfeit the sum of forty shillings, and every driver or conductor charged with such offence, who, when required by a justice of the peace so to do, shall not truly make known the name and place of abode of the person so suffered by him to act as driver or conductor without the consent of the proprietor, and also the number of the ticket of such person (if licensed), shall be liable to a further penalty of forty shillings, and it shall be lawful for any police constable, without any warrant for that purpose, to take into custody any person unlawfully acting as a driver or as a conductor, and to convey him before any justice of the peace, to be dealt with according to law, and also, if necessary, to take charge of the carriage and every horse in charge of such person, and to deposit the same in some place of safe custody until the same can be applied for by the proprietor. *No person to act as driver of any carriage without the consent of the proprietor.*

28. Every driver of a hackney carriage, or driver or conductor of a metropolitan stage carriage, who shall be guilty of wanton or furious driving, or who by carelessness or wilful misbehaviour shall cause any hurt or damage to any person or property being in any street or highway, and also every driver or conductor . who during his employment shall be drunk, or shall make use of any insulting or abusive language, or shall be guilty of any insulting gesture or any misbehaviour, shall for every such offence forfeit *Punishment for furious driving and wilful misbehaviour*

the sum of three pounds, or it shall be lawful for the justice before whom such complaint shall be brought, if in his discretion he shall think proper, instead of inflicting such penalty forthwith, to commit the offender to prison for any period not exceeding two calendar months, with or without hard labour as the justice shall direct; and in every case where any such hurt or damage shall have been caused the justice, upon the hearing of the complaint, may adjudge, as and for compensation to any party aggrieved as aforesaid, a sum not exceeding ten pounds, and may order the proprietor of the hackney carriage or metropolitan stage carriage the driver or conductor of which shall have caused such hurt or damage forthwith to pay such sum, and also such costs as shall have been incurred, and payment thereof may be enforced against such proprietor as any penalty or sum of money may be recovered under and by virtue of this Act, and any sum which shall be so paid by the proprietor shall in like manner be recovered in a summary way before a justice of the peace from the driver or conductor through whose default such sum shall have been paid, upon proof of the payment thereof, pursuant to the order of the justice, or it shall be lawful for the justice in the first instance to adjudge the amount of such compensation to be paid by such driver or conductor to the party aggrieved

<small>Standings to be appointed</small>

29. It shall be lawful for the Commissioners of Police of the Metropolis from time to time to make regulations for enforcing order at the places at which metropolitan stage carriages shall call or ply for passengers, and for fixing the time during which each such carriage shall be allowed to remain at any such place, and . every driver or conductor of a metropolitan stage carriage who shall wilfully disregard or not conform himself to such regulations shall for every such offence forfeit the sum of forty shillings

<small>Standings to be in the centre of streets</small>

30. No standing shall be appointed for hackney carriages, either within the Metropolitan Police District or within the City of London, by virtue of this Act or of any other Act, except in the centre part of the street, unless in the case of a street with houses only on one side of such street

<small>Hackney carriages not to ply opposite General Post Office</small>

31. Nothing herein or in any other Act contained shall be deemed or construed to authorise any hackney carriage to stand or ply for hire opposite to the General Post Office in Saint Martin's-le-Grand, London, or any part thereof

32. It shall be lawful for the Court of Mayor and Aldermen of the City of London within the City of London and the liberties thereof, and the Borough of Southwark, to make regulations for enforcing order at the places at which metropolitan stage carriages shall call or ply for passengers, and for fixing the time during which each such carriage shall be allowed to remain at any such place, and every driver or conductor of a metropolitan stage carriage who shall wilfully disregard or not conform himself to such regulations shall forfeit the sum of forty shillings

Lord Mayor and Aldermen to make regulations with respect to carriages &c in the City and the Borough

33. Every driver of a hackney carriage who shall ply for hire elsewhere than at some standing or place appointed for that purpose, or who by loitering or by any wilful misbehaviour shall cause any obstruction in or upon any public street, road, or place, and also every driver or conductor of any metropolitan stage carriage who by loitering or any wilful misbehaviour shall cause any obstruction in or upon any public street, road, or place, or shall improperly delay such carriage on any journey, or wilfully deceive any person in respect to the route or destination thereof, or who shall refuse to admit and carry at the lawful fare any passenger for whom there is room, and to whose admission no reasonable objection is made, or who shall demand more than the legal fare for any passenger, or who, for the purpose of taking up or setting down a passenger, or, except in case of accident or other unavoidable necessity, shall stop such carriage opposite to the end of any street, or upon any place where foot passengers usually cross the carriage-way, or who shall ply for hire or passengers by blowing a horn, or by using any other noisy instrument, within the limits of the Metropolis as defined by the said Act of the second year of the reign of His late Majesty, and every conductor of a metropolitan stage carriage who shall allow any person beside himself to ride upon the steps or in the place provided for him, and every driver of a hackney carriage, whether hired or unhired, allowing any person besides himself, not being the hirer or a person employed by such hirer, to ride on the driving box, and every driver or conductor of any metropolitan stage carriage who shall smoke whilst acting in such capacity, after an objection taken by any person riding in or upon such carriage, shall for every such offence forfeit the sum of twenty shillings

Penalty on drivers of hackney carriages, or drivers or conductors of metropolitan stage carriages, for loitering or causing any obstruction, or plying for hire by making any noise &c

34. *Repealed*

Proprietors may be summoned to appear and produce the driver or conductor

35. When any complaint shall be made before any justice of the peace against the driver of any hackney carriage, or the driver or the conductor of any metropolitan stage carriage, for any offence committed by him against the provisions of this Act, or of the recited Act of His late Majesty, or of any order or regulations made in pursuance of this Act, it shall be lawful for such justice, if he shall think proper, forthwith to summon the proprietor of such carriage to produce before him, or such other justice of the peace as shall be then present, the driver or conductor by whom such offence was committed to answer such complaint, and in case such proprietor, after being duly summoned, shall fail to produce the driver or conductor, it shall be lawful for the justice of the peace before whom such driver or conductor should be produced (if he shall think fit) to proceed, in the absence of such driver or conductor, to hear and determine the case in the same manner as if he had been produced, and to adjudge payment by the proprietor of any penalty or sum of money and costs in which the driver shall be convicted, and any sum of money which shall be so paid by the proprietor shall be recovered in a summary way from the driver or conductor by whose default such sum shall have been paid upon proof of payment thereof, pursuant to the order of the justice, and upon proof of the service of the notice hereinafter mentioned

In case of proprietors failing so to do.

Provided always, that if the justice of the peace shall deem it proper, it shall be lawful for him when such proprietor shall fail to produce his driver or conductor, without any satisfactory excuse to be allowed by such justice, to impose a fine of forty shillings upon such proprietor, and so from time to time as often as he shall be summoned in respect of such complaint until he shall produce his driver and conductor, and every proprietor so summoned to produce his driver or conductor shall cause to be given to such driver or conductor, or to be left at the abode specified in his licence, or (if such licence shall expire after the offence committed and before the hearing of the complaint) at his usual place of abode, a written notice of the time and place when and where such driver or conductor shall be required to attend, and if such driver or conductor shall not attend according to such notice, it shall be lawful for a justice of the peace to issue a warrant for his apprehension, and if after such notice any driver or conductor shall, without a reasonable excuse to be allowed by the justice, neglect or refuse to attend at the time and place therein mentioned, or (having previously left the service of the proprietor so summoned as aforesaid) shall not at the time and place of his attendance produce his licence, he shall forfeit the sum of forty shillings, and so from time to time as often as he shall so neglect or refuse.

36. It shall be lawful for any magistrate specially appointed under the authority of the said Act of the reign of His late Majesty for the purpose of hearing and determining offences against the provisions of that Act, or for such other magistrate as shall be in attendance at the office appointed in that behalf, to hear and determine any complaint for any offence against the provisions of this Act, or of any Act now in force or hereafter to be in force, wheresoever the cause of complaint may arise, within the City of London or the liberties thereof, or elsewhere within the limits of this Act, so far as the same shall relate to hackney carriages or to metropolitan stage carriages, in like manner as if such provisions had been included in the aforesaid Act. *Magistrates empowered to hear and determine complaints*

37. Upon the hearing of any complaint made under the provisions of this Act or the recited Act passed in the reign of His late Majesty, or of the orders and regulations aforesaid, it shall be lawful for the justice of the peace by whom the same shall be heard to examine and take the evidence of the informant or complainant in any dispute concerning the amount of fare paid or demanded by either party, or in any dispute between the proprietor and driver or conductor of any hackney carriage or metropolitan stage carriage concerning the wages of such driver or conductor, or in any complaint of personal injury done to the complainant by the driver of any hackney carriage or metropolitan stage carriage, or in any case in which the informant or complainant shall be entitled to no pecuniary advantage besides his costs and expenses, or, being entitled to some compensation or pecuniary advantage, shall either give up all claim to the same, or shall not be the only witness in the case. *Evidence of complainant to be taken*

38. All complaints under the provisions of the said recited Act of the reign of His late Majesty or of this Act, or of the orders and regulations made in pursuance of either of them, except such as shall be made by the direction of the Commissioners of Stamps and Taxes, and except in cases where some other term of limitation is specially provided by this Act, shall be made within seven days next after the day on which the cause of complaint shall have arisen. *Complaints to be made within seven days*

Penalties may be awarded to be paid by instalments

In case of nonpayment the party may be imprisoned

Proviso

39. It shall be lawful for any justice of the peace to hear and determine all complaints under the provisions of this Act or of the said recited Act of the reign of His late Majesty, and to adjudge the payment of any penalty or of any sum of money under either of the said Acts, or of the orders and regulations made pursuant to either of them, and to order payment of the same, with or without costs, either immediately or at such time and place, and by such instalments, as he shall think fit; and in case of nonpayment of the sum so ordered to be paid, or of any one instalment thereof, to adjudge the party making default to be imprisoned in the common gaol or house of correction for any term not exceeding two calendar months, with or without hard labour, such imprisonment to cease on payment of the sum so adjudged or ordered to be paid, or to issue his warrant for the levying any such sum of money, together with the costs and expenses of such warrant or of levying the same, on the goods of the party making default, and to cause sale to be made of such goods in case they shall not be redeemed within five days, rendering to the party the overplus (if any), and where goods of such party making default cannot be found sufficient to answer the penalty or sum ordered to be paid, and all such costs and expenses, to commit such party to prison, there to remain for any time not exceeding two calendar months, unless such penalty or sum of money, and all such costs and expenses, shall be sooner paid; and every such imprisonment shall be with or without hard labour as such justice shall direct. Provided always that no imprisonment for nonpayment of any sum ordered to be paid on account of wages, or the earnings of any carriage or of any deposit of money, shall be for a longer period than one calendar month, or with hard labour; and all proceedings whatsoever before any justice of the peace under any of the provisions of this Act or the recited Act of the reign of His late Majesty, and the judgment of the said justice thereon, shall be final and conclusive between the parties, and shall not be quashed or vacated for want of form, and shall not be removed by *certiorari*, or any other writ or process, into any other superior Court.

In what manner goods distrained under this Act shall be sold

40. In all cases where any goods or chattels distrained or otherwise seized or taken under any of the provisions of this Act or the recited Act of the late reign are directed to be sold, the same shall be sold by public auction, and notice of the time and place of such sale shall be given to the owner of such goods and chattels, or left at his usual place of abode,

three days at least prior to such sale Provided always that if the owner of any such goods and chattels shall give his consent in writing to the sale thereof at an earlier period than is by this Act or shall be by any such notice appointed for such sale, or in any other manner than is by this Act directed, it shall be lawful to sell such goods or chattels according to such consent Provided also, that if the owner of such goods or chattels shall, at any time before the sale thereof, pay or tender to the person who by any warrant or other process shall be directed or authorised to cause such goods or chattels to be sold the sum which he shall by such warrant or process be directed to levy or raise by the sale of such goods or chattels, together with all reasonable costs and expenses incurred, no sale of such goods or chattels shall be made

41. For the purpose of serving summonses and other notices required by this or the recited Act of His late Majesty the usual place of abode of any driver, conductor or of any person who, having been licensed as a driver or conductor .. has neglected to return his metal ticket at the expiration of his licence, shall be deemed to be the place specified in the licence, and it shall be lawful for any justice of the peace in all cases, upon complaint being made in respect of any matter within the meaning of this or of the recited Act of His late Majesty, or of the orders and regulations made in pursuance thereof, to issue his summons to require the attendance of the person complained of before the said justice, or any other justice, at a time and place to be appointed for that purpose, or to issue a warrant for the apprehension of such person, either in the first instance, or after the issuing and service of such summons and the non-appearance of the party summoned, and every summons or other notice required by this Act shall be deemed to be duly served, provided the same, or a copy thereof, shall be either personally served or left at the usual place of abode of the party to whom it shall be directed, or if he shall be a party licensed under this or the recited Act of His late Majesty, then at the place of abode specified in his licence *Service of summonses and other notices*

42. Every person summoned as a witness to give evidence touching any matter to be heard under this Act or the recited Act of His late Majesty, who shall neglect or refuse to appear at the time and place for that purpose appointed by any justice of the peace, without a reasonable excuse to be allowed by such justice, or who shall appear but refuse to be examined or give evidence, shall forfeit the sum of five pounds *Penalty on witnesses refusing to attend or to give evidence.*

Certain proceedings to be drawn up according to the forms in the schedule.

43. Every summons or warrant of distress which shall be had or taken against the proprietor of a hackney carriage or metropolitan stage carriage, for the default of the driver or conductor thereof, for the recovery of any penalty, compensation, or costs under the provisions of this Act, or such rules, orders, and regulations as aforesaid, may be drawn or made out according to the several forms contained in the schedule hereunto annexed, or to the effect thereof, with such changes as the case may require, and every order, conviction, warrant, or other proceeding which shall be drawn, had, or issued under the provisions of this Act or of the recited Act of the reign of His late Majesty, or of such rules, orders, and regulations as aforesaid, shall be good and effectual without stating the facts in evidence, or more than the matter of offence in respect whereof such order, conviction, or other proceeding as aforesaid shall have been had, made or issued

Providing for cases where there are more proprietors than one

44. In every case where there shall be more than one proprietor of any hackney carriage or metropolitan stage carriage, it shall be sufficient, in any information, summons, order, conviction, warrant, or any other proceeding under the provisions of this Act or of the said recited Act of the reign of His late Majesty, to name one of such proprietors without reference to any other or others of them, and to describe and proceed against him as if he were sole proprietor

Power to mitigate penalties

45. It shall be lawful for any justice of the peace by whom any person shall be convicted of any offence under this Act, or under the recited Act of His late Majesty, to lessen the penalty or term of imprisonment in such manner as he may think fit

Appropriation of penalties.

46. All penalties or sums of money ordered and adjudged within the Metropolitan Police District to be paid under this Act or the recited Act of His late Majesty, and not otherwise appropriated, shall be payable to Her Majesty, and all penalties or sums of money ordered and adjudged within the City of London or the liberties thereof to be paid under this Act or the recited Act of His late Majesty, and not otherwise appropriated, shall be payable to the Chamberlain of the City of London, in aid of the expenses of the police of the said city

47 and 48. *Repealed*

SCHEDULE REFERRED TO IN THE FOREGOING ACT

No. 1.

Form of a Summons to the Proprietor of a Hackney Carriage or a Metropolitan Stage Carriage to produce the Driver or Conductor thereof to answer a Complaint

To E F, of &c, proprietor of the hackney carriage number   [or the metropolitan stage carriage number   ]

Whereas complaint hath been made by C D against the driver of the hackney carriage number   [or the driver or conductor of the metropolitan stage carriage number   ] on the   day of   now last passed [or instant], charging that the said driver [or conductor], on the   day of   now last passed [or instant] (of which said carriage you were then the proprietor), at or about the hour of   did [*here state the alleged offence*] These are therefore to require you to produce the said driver [or conductor] before me, or such other magistrate as shall be present, at   on the   day of   at   of the clock in the   noon, then and there to answer the said complaint

Dated the   day of   .

(Signed)
One of the Police Magistrates of the Metropolis
[or
One of Her Majesty's Justices of the Peace for   ]

No. 2.

Form of a Warrant of Distress for levying upon the Proprietor of a Hackney Carriage or Metropolitan Stage Carriage the Penalty in which the Driver or Conductor thereof has been convicted

To *A B*, of &c.

Metropolitan Police District to wit

Whereas *C D*, the driver of the hackney carriage number   [or the driver or conductor of the metropolitan stage carriage number   ], on the   day of   was duly convicted of a certain offence, for that [*here state the offence*], whereby he hath been adjudged to forfeit the sum of   , over and above the sum of   for the costs and charges of the informer, making together the sum of   which hath not been paid by the said driver [or conductor], nor by any person on his behalf. And whereas, according to the statute in that behalf made, the said *E F*, the proprietor of the said carriage, hath been required to pay the said sum of   , which he hath neglected and refused to do. Therefore I command you to levy the said sum of   by distraining the goods and chattels of the said *E F*, the said proprietor, and if within the space of five days next after such distress taken the said sum of   , together with the reasonable costs and charges of taking and keeping such distress, shall not be paid, then I order and direct that you shall sell and dispose of the said goods and chattels which shall be so distrained, taken, and seized as aforesaid, and shall levy and raise thereout the said sum of   and all reasonable costs and charges of taking and keeping and selling such distress, rendering the overplus (if any) to the owner of the said goods and chattels, and you are to certify to me what you shall have done by virtue of this my warrant.

Given under my hand and seal the   day of

(Signed)
One of the Police Magistrates of the Metropolis
[*or*
One of Her Majesty's Justices of the Peace for   ]

No. 3.

Form of Warrant of Commitment of the Proprietor of a Hackney Carriage or Metropolitan Stage Carriage for want of a sufficient Distress whereon to levy the Penalty in which the Driver or Conductor of such Carriage has been convicted

To A B, of &c, and to the Keeper of the Common Gaol [or House of Correction] at

Metropolitan Police District to wit

Whereas &c [*proceed as in the Form No 2 to the words* "which he hath neglected and refused to do," *inclusive*] And whereas it has been duly made to appear to me that no sufficient distress of the goods and chattels of the said E F, the said proprietor, can be found whereon to levy the said sum of   Therefore I command you the said A B to apprehend and take the said E F., and safely to convey him to the common gaol [or house of correction] at   in the   of   and there to deliver him to the keeper thereof, together with this warrant   And I do hereby command you the said keeper to receive into your custody in the said gaol [or house of correction] him the said E F, and him therein safely to keep for the space of   unless the said sum of   shall be sooner paid.

Given under my hand and seal the   day of   .

(Signed)
One of the Police Magistrates of the Metropolis
[*or*
One of Her Majesty's Justices of the Peace for   ]

THE LONDON HACKNEY CARRIAGES ACT, 1850.

(13-4 V 7)

An Act for consolidating the Office of the Registrar of Metropolitan Public Carriages with the Office of Commissioners of Police of the Metropolis, and making other provisions in regard to the consolidated Offices [25th March, 1850

1. *Repealed*

Duties of abolished office transferred to Commissioners of Police

2. All the jurisdiction, powers, authorities, privileges, interests, and duties now vested in or exercised by the office of Registrar of Metropolitan Public Carriages hereby abolished shall be transferred to and vested in and shall hereafter be exercised by the Commissioners of Police of the Metropolis, in as full and ample a manner to all intents and purposes as they were vested in and might have been exercised by the said Registrar of Metropolitan Public Carriages

3. *Repealed*

Standings for hackney carriages to be appointed

4. It shall be lawful for the said Commissioners of Police from time to time to appoint standings for hackney carriages at such places as they shall think convenient in any street, thoroughfare, or place of public resort within the Metropolitan Police District, any law, statute, or custom to the contrary thereof notwithstanding, and at their discretion to alter the same, and from time to time to make regulations concerning the boundaries of the same, and the number of carriages to be allowed at any such standing, and the times at and during which they may stand and ply for hire at any such standing, and also from time to time to make such regulations as the said Commissioners shall deem proper for enforcing order at every such standing, and for removing any person who shall unnecessarily loiter or remain at or about any such standing, and the said Commissioners shall cause all the orders and regulations to be made by them as aforesaid to be advertised in the *London Gazette*, and a copy thereof, signed by one of the said Commissioners, to be hung up for public inspection in the office of the Commissioners of Police in the City of Westminster and at each of the police courts, and such copy shall be received in evidence in the said courts as if it were the original of which it purports to be a copy, and shall be taken to be a true copy of such original order or regulation, without further proof than the signature of the said Commissioner [*sic*]

5. *Repealed*

6. Provided always nothing in this Act or in the said Act of the seventh year of the reign of Her present Majesty contained shall alter or repeal, or be construed to alter or repeal, or invalidate, or in anywise prejudicially affect, either wholly or in part, an Act passed in the forty-sixth year of the reign of His Majesty King George the Third, intituled "An Act for ornamenting and embellishing the centre or area of Bloomsbury Square, in the parish of Saint George, Bloomsbury, in the County of Middlesex, and for preventing hackney coaches standing or plying for hire in or near the said Square" {Saving of Bloomsbury Square Act, 46 G. III. c. cxxxiv}

7. *Repealed*

8. This Act shall be construed as one Act with the said Act passed in the seventh year of the reign of Her Majesty Queen Victoria, intituled "An Act for regulating Hackney and Stage Carriages in and near London," and that all the provisions of the said Act, except so far as is herein otherwise provided, shall extend to this Act, and to all things done in execution of this Act. {This Act to be construed with 6 & 7 Vict c. 86.}

9 and 10. *Repealed*

THE LONDON HACKNEY CARRIAGES ACT, 1853.

(16-7 V 33)

An Act for the better Regulation of Metropolitan Stage and Hackney Carriages, and for prohibiting the use of Advertising Vehicles.

[28th June, 1853

1. *Repealed*

Commissioners of Police may cause carriages &c to be inspected, and if not in fit condition may suspend licences, and recall stamp office plate.

2. It shall be lawful for the said Commissioners of Police to cause an inspection to be made, as often as they deem it necessary, of all metropolitan stage and hackney carriages, and of the horse or horses used in drawing the same, within the limits of this Act, and if any such carriage, or the horse or horses used in drawing the same, shall at any time be in a condition unfit for public use, the said Commissioners shall give notice in writing accordingly to the proprietor thereof, which notice shall be personally served on such proprietor, or delivered at his usual place of residence, and if, after notice as aforesaid, any proprietor shall use or let to hire such carriage as a metropolitan stage or hackney carriage, or use or let to hire such horse or horses whilst in a condition unfit for public use, the said Commissioners shall have power to suspend, for such time as they may deem proper, the licence of the proprietor of such carriage

3. *Repealed*

As to rates and fares to be taken for hackney carriages

4. The proprietor or driver of any hackney carriage within the limits of this Act shall be entitled to demand and take for hire of such carriage the fares set forth in the Schedule (A) to this Act annexed Provided always that when the proprietor or driver of any hackney carriage to be paid a fare calculated according to the distance shall be required by the hirer thereof to stop such carriage for fifteen minutes, or for any longer time, it shall be lawful for the proprietor or driver to demand and receive from the hirer so requiring him to stop a further sum (above the fare to which he shall be entitled, calculated according to the distance) of sixpence for every fifteen minutes completed that he shall have been so stopped, and no proprietor or driver shall demand or receive over and above the said fare any sum, for or by way of back fare, for the return of such carriage from the place at which such carriage shall be discharged

No back fare to be taken or demanded.

5. The driver of every hackney carriage within the limits of this Act shall have with him at all times when plying for hire a book or table in such form as shall be directed by the said Commissioners of Police of the fares for the hire of such carriage, which book or table the driver shall produce when required for the information of any person hiring or intending to hire such carriage

Driver to produce book of fares when required.

6. In case of disputes as to the fare to be calculated according to the distance, any table or book signed by the said Commissioners of Police shall, on proof of such signature, be deemed and taken to be conclusive evidence of all the distances therein stated to have been measured by the authority of the said Commissioners of Police, and it shall be lawful for the said Commissioners to cause to be placed or erected at the several standings for hackney carriages or elsewhere within the Metropolitan District, as they may deem convenient, tables of distances and fares, and such other information as may be useful to persons hiring such carriage

As to settlement of disputes as to distances.

7. The driver of every hackney carriage which shall ply for hire at any place within the limits of this Act shall (unless such driver have a reasonable excuse, to be allowed by the justice before whom the matter shall be brought in question) drive such hackney carriage to any place to which he shall be required by the hirer thereof to drive the same, not exceeding six miles from the place where the same shall have been hired, or for any time not exceeding one hour from the time when hired. Provided always that when any hackney carriage shall have been hired by time, the driver thereof may be required to drive at any rate not exceeding four miles within one hour, and if the driver of such carriage shall be required to drive more than four miles within one hour, then in every such case the driver thereof shall be entitled to demand, in addition to the fare regulated by time in Schedule (A) to this Act annexed, for every mile or any part thereof exceeding four miles, the fare regulated by distance as set forth in the same Schedule

As to distance drivers of hackney carriages shall be required to drive.

8. *Repealed.*

Number of persons to to be carried
9. . The driver of any such hackney carriage shall, if required by the hirer thereof, carry in and by such carriage the number of persons painted or marked thereon, or any less number of persons

As to quantity of luggage to be carried without extra charge
10. The driver of every hackney carriage within the limits of this Act shall carry in or upon such carriage a reasonable quantity of luggage for every person hiring such carriage without any additional charge, except as provided in Schedule (A) to this Act annexed.

Property left in hackney carriages to be deposited at the police office

Penalty on driver for default

Property not claimed to be disposed of

Penalty on refusing or neglecting to give up property left in stage carriages

11. The driver of every hackney carriage within the limits of this Act wherein any property shall be left by any person shall, within twenty-four hours, carry such property, if not sooner claimed by the owner thereof, in the state in which he shall find the same, to the nearest police station, and shall there deposit and leave the same with the inspector or other officer on duty, upon pain that every such driver making any such default herein shall be liable to a penalty not more than ten pounds, or at the discretion of the magistrate may be imprisoned for any time not exceeding one month, and the said officer with whom any such property shall be deposited shall forthwith enter in a book to be kept for that purpose the description of such property, and the name and address of the driver who shall bring the same, and the day on which it shall be brought; and the property so entered shall be returned to the person who shall prove, to the satisfaction of the Commissioners of Police, that the same belonged to him, such person previously paying all expenses incurred, together with such reasonable sum to the driver who brought the same as the said Commissioners shall award Provided always, that if such property shall not be claimed by and proved to belong to some person within one year after the same shall have been deposited, the said Commissioners shall cause such property to be sold or otherwise disposed of, and the proceeds thereof to be paid over to the Receiver-General of Inland Revenue, to be carried to the public account, all expenses incurred about such property, together with such reasonable sum to the driver who brought the same as the said Commissioners shall award, being first paid thereout, and all property left by any passenger in any metropolitan stage carriage shall be given up to the conductor of such carriage, or, if there be no conductor, to the driver, upon pain of a penalty of ten pounds, to be paid by any person refusing or neglecting to give up any such property belonging to another person, and the conductor or driver of every such carriage to whom any such property shall be given up, or who shall himself find it in the carriage, shall within twenty-four hours carry the property, if not sooner claimed by the owner thereof, in the state in which he shall find the same to the nearest police station, and shall there deposit and leave the same with the inspector or other officer on duty, upon pain that every such driver or conductor making default herein shall be liable to a penalty not more than ten pounds, or at the discretion of a magistrate may be imprisoned for any time not exceeding one month, and the property so deposited by any conductor or driver shall be dealt with in the same manner as property left in carriages and deposited by the drivers of such carriages

12. It shall be lawful for the said Commissioners of Police from time to time to appoint a sufficient number of fit men to enforce good order at the standings for hackney carriages, and at the places at which metropolitan stage carriages or hackney carriages shall call or ply for passengers, and at such places of public resort within the Metropolitan Police District as they may deem necessary, and the said Commissioners may from time to time make such orders and regulations as they shall deem expedient, subject to the approval of one of Her Majesty's Principal Secretaries of State given in writing, relative to the duties to be performed by such persons and the places at which each shall act provided that the said Commissioners shall not have authority to appoint any such person to act within or upon the premises belonging to any railway company unless with the consent of the directors of the company

Commissioners of Police to appoint persons to enforce good order at hackney carriage stands &c

13. The said Commissioners of Police, subject to the approbation of the Treasury, shall appoint wages to be paid to the said persons appointed by them to keep good order at the standings for hackney carriages and at the places at which metropolitan stage carriages or hackney carriages shall call or ply for passengers, and at such places of public resort as they may deem necessary, and the said Commissioners shall also, in such cases as they think fit, direct the water rates and the expenses of the necessary apparatus for laying on the water at the standings for hackney carriages and at places where metropolitan stage carriages usually call or ply for hire to be paid

Power to Commissioners, with consent of Treasury, to pay wages to such persons, and also to direct water rates to be paid

Lamps to be placed inside metropolitan stage carriages

14. The proprietor of every metropolitan stage carriage shall cause to be placed inside such carriage a lamp, in such a position and manner as shall be directed by the said Commissioners of Police, and the conductor, or if there be no conductor the driver of such carriage shall keep the said lamp properly lighted whenever such carriage shall be used to ply for hire or carry passengers at any time after sunset and before sunrise

Printed bills &c not to be put on metropolitan stage or hackney carriages, so as to obstruct light &c

15. It shall not be lawful for the proprietor of any metropolitan stage or hackney carriage to suffer any notice, advertisement, or printed bill, or any names, letters, or numbers, to appear upon the outside of any such carriage in such a manner as to obstruct the light or ventilation of such carriage, or on the inside of any such carriage in such position that any such notice, advertisement, or printed bill shall obstruct the light or ventilation of such carriage or cause annoyance to any passenger therein

Advertising vehicles &c prohibited

16. It shall not be lawful for any person to carry about on any carriage or on horseback or on foot, in any thoroughfare or public place within the limits of this Act, to the obstruction or annoyance of the inhabitants or passengers, any picture, placard, notice, or advertisement, whether written, printed, or painted upon or posted or attached to any part of such carriage, or any board, or otherwise.

Drivers and conductors of metropolitan stage carriages and drivers of hackney carriages liable to penalties for offences herein named

17. The driver or conductor of any metropolitan stage carriage, or the driver of any hackney carriage, who shall respectively commit any of the following offences within the limits of this Act, shall be liable to a penalty not exceeding forty shillings for each offence, or in default of payment to imprisonment

1 Every driver of a hackney carriage who shall demand or take more than the proper fare as set forth in Schedule A to this Act annexed, or who shall refuse to admit and carry in his carriage the number of persons painted or marked on such carriage or specified in the certificate granted by the said Commissioners of Police in respect of such carriage, or who shall refuse to carry by his carriage a reasonable quantity of luggage for any person hiring or intending to hire such carriage

2 Every driver of a hackney carriage who shall refuse to drive such carriage to any place within the limits of this Act, not exceeding six miles, to which he shall be required to drive any person hiring or

intending to hire such carriage, or who shall refuse to drive any such carriage for any time not exceeding one hour, if so required by any person hiring or intending to hire such carriage, or who shall not drive the same at a reasonable and proper speed, not less than six miles an hour, except in cases of unavoidable delay, or when required by the hirer thereof to drive at any slower pace

3. Every driver of a hackney carriage who shall ply for hire with any carriage or horse which shall be at the time unfit for public use . . .

18. It shall be lawful for any one of the police magistrates at any of the Metropolitan Police Courts to hear and determine all offences against the provisions of this Act, and also all disputes or causes of complaint that may arise out of the same, or if the offence, dispute, or cause of complaint shall be committed or occur in any place not comprised within the limits of a police court district, the same may be heard and determined by two justices of the peace for the county, or if the offence, dispute, or cause of complaint shall be committed or occur within the City of London, the same shall be heard and determined by one justice of the peace for the said City, or by a metropolitan police magistrate sitting at the police court in Bow Street . . *Power to police magistrates or justices of the peace to hear and determine offences.*

19. For every offence against the provisions of this Act for which no special penalty is hereinbefore appointed, the offender shall be liable to a penalty not exceeding forty shillings, or in default of payment be imprisoned *Penalty for offences against this Act for which no penalty is appointed*

20. All things herein authorised to be done by the said Commissioners of Police of the Metropolis shall be done by such one of the said Commissioners as one of Her Majesty's Principal Secretaries of State shall from time to time be pleased to appoint, and the words "the limits of this Act" shall include every part of the Metropolitan Police District and City of London. *Meaning of certain words used in this Act.*

21. This Act shall be construed as one Act with the Act passed in the seventh year of the reign of Her Majesty Queen Victoria, chapter eighty-six, and the Act passed in the thirteenth year of the reign of Her Majesty, chapter seven, and all the provisions of the said Acts, except so far as is herein otherwise provided, shall extend to this Act, and to all things done in execution of this Act *This Act to be construed with 6 & 7 Vict c. 86, and 13 & 14 Vict. c 7*

22. *Repealed*

SCHEDULES REFERRED TO IN THE FOREGOING ACT

Rates and Fares to be paid for any Hackney Carriage hired at any place within the Limits of this Act

SCHEDULE A.

Description of Carriage	Fare by Distance		Fare by Time	
	For any Distance within and not exceeding One Mile	For any Distance exceeding One Mile	For any Time within and not exceeding One Hour	
With Four or Two Wheels, drawn by One Horse	6d	After the Rate of Sixpence for every Mile, and for any part of a Mile over and above any Number of Miles completed	2s	And for every Hackney Carriage drawn by Two Horses One Third above the Rates and Fares hereinbefore mentioned

The above fares to be paid according to distance or time, at the option of the hirer, to be expressed at the commencement of the hiring, if not otherwise expressed, the fares to be paid according to distance

Provided that no driver shall be compellable to hire his carriage for a fare to be paid according to time at any time after eight o'clock in the evening and before six o'clock in the morning

When more than two persons shall be carried inside any hackney carriage, one sum of sixpence is to be paid for the whole hiring in addition to the above fares Two children under ten years of age to be counted as one adult person

When more than two persons shall be carried inside any hackney carriage with more luggage than can be carried inside the carriage a further sum of twopence for every package carried outside the said carriage is to be paid by the hirer in addition to the above fares

Schedules B and C. *Repealed*

THE LONDON HACKNEY CARRIAGES ACT, 1853.

(16-7 V 127)

An Act . . . . . to make provision as to the Charge for the Hire of Hackney Carriages in certain Cases [20th August, 1853.

1 to 12. *Repealed*

13. It shall be lawful for the driver of any hackney carriage within the limits of this Act to charge one shilling per mile for every mile (or part of a mile) which he shall be required to drive beyond the circumference of a circle the radius of which shall be four miles from Charing Cross, provided such carriage shall be discharged beyond such circumference, anything contained in the thirty-third chapter of an Act of the sixteenth and seventeenth year of the reign of Her present Majesty, or in the schedule thereto, notwithstanding

1s. a mile to be paid for every mile beyond the circumference of a circle four miles from Charing Cross if carriage be discharged beyond such circumference

14. Whenever more than two persons shall be conveyed by any hackney carriage drawn by one horse only, a sum of sixpence for each person above the number of two shall be paid for the whole hiring in addition to the fare now directed to be paid for two persons under the said Act of the sixteenth and seventeenth year of the reign of Her present Majesty, chapter thirty three; and two children under ten years old shall be considered as one adult person for the purposes of this clause

Where more than two persons are conveyed in a hackney carriage drawn by one horse, 6d. in addition to the fare to be paid for each person above two for the whole hiring

When carriage hired by time 6d to be paid for every fifteen minutes, or portion thereof, over the hour

15. When any hackney carriage within the limits of this Act hired for a fare to be paid according to time shall be hired or used by the hirer thereof for any longer time than one hour, sixpence shall be paid for every fifteen minutes, or any portion of fifteen minutes not completed, above one hour.

Proprietors of hackney carriages withdrawing carriages from hire beyond a certain time liable to a penalty.

16. The proprietor of every hackney carriage or metropolitan stage carriage licensed to ply for hire within the limits of this Act who shall withdraw his carriage from hire for two consecutive days, or for any two days in one week, without just cause, of which the magistrate before whom the complaint is heard shall be the judge, shall be liable to a penalty of a sum not exceeding twenty shillings in respect of every carriage for each day he shall so withdraw the same, and the licence of such proprietor shall be suspended or recalled and taken away at the discretion of the said Commissioners of Police Provided always that it shall be lawful for such proprietor, upon giving ten days' notice to the Commissioners of Police, to withdraw his carriage from hire

"The limits of this Act" defined

17. The limits of this Act shall be deemed to be and to include every part of the Metropolitan Police District and the City of London, and all provisions of any former Act in force referring to hackney carriages licensed under the said Act of the first and second years of His late Majesty, or to hackney carriages kept, used, employed, or let to hire within the distance of five miles from the General Post Office in the City of London, or to any act, matter, or thing committed or done in relation to such hackney carriages within the said distance, shall from and after the passing of this Act be deemed to refer and apply to hackney carriages licensed under this Act, or to hackney carriages, kept, used, employed, or let to hire within the limits of this Act, and to any act, matter, or thing committed or done in relation to hackney carriages within the said limits

18. *Repealed.*

THE METROPOLITAN PUBLIC CARRIAGE ACT, 1869.

(32-3 V. 115.)

An Act for amending the Law relating to Hackney and Stage Carriages within the Metropolitan Police District   [11th August, 1869

1. This Act may be cited for all purposes as "The Metropolitan Public Carriage Act, 1869" — *Short title*

2. The limits of this Act shall be the Metropolitan Police District and the City of London and the liberties thereof — *Limits of Act.*

3. *Repealed.*

4. In this Act "stage carriage" shall mean any carriage for the conveyance of passengers which plies for hire in any public street, road, or place within the limits of this Act, and in which the passengers or any of them are charged to pay separate and distinct, or at the rate of separate and distinct, fares for their respective places or seats therein. — *Definition of "stage carriage" and "hackney carriage"*

"Hackney carriage" shall mean any carriage for the conveyance of passengers which plies for hire within the limits of this Act, and is not a stage carriage

"Prescribed" shall mean "prescribed by order of one of Her Majesty's Principal Secretaries of State" — *Meaning of "prescribed."*

5. A "stage carriage" which on every journey goes to or comes from some town or place beyond the limits of this Act shall not be deemed to be a carriage plying within the limits of this Act — *Exemption of certain carriages from operations of Act.*

Licensing Hackney and Stage Carriages

6. One of Her Majesty's Principal Secretaries of State may from time to time license to ply for hire within the limits of this Act hackney and stage carriages, to be distinguished in such manner as he may by order prescribe. — *Grant of hackney carriage licences.*

Any licence in respect of a hackney or stage carriage under this section may be granted at such price, on such conditions, be in such form, be subject to such revision or suspension in such events, and generally be dealt in such manner as the Secretary of State may by order prescribe, subject as follows —

(1) That a hackney or stage carriage licence shall, if not revoked or suspended, be in force for one year, and there shall be paid in respect thereof to the Receiver of the Metropolitan Police, to be carried to the account of the Metropolitan Police Fund, such uniform sum, not exceeding two pounds two shillings, as the Secretary of State may prescribe

(2) That in any such order provision shall be made for the transfer of a hackney or stage carriage licence to the widow or to any child of full age of any person to whom a hackney or stage carriage licence has been granted who may die during the continuance of such licence leaving a widow or child of full age, and also for the transfer of a hackney or stage carriage licence to the husband of any woman to whom such licence has been granted, and who marries during the continuance thereof

Penalty on use of unlicensed carriage

7. If any unlicensed hackney or stage carriage plies for hire, the owner of such carriage shall be liable to a penalty not exceeding five pounds for every day during which such unlicensed carriage plies And if any unlicensed hackney carriage is found on any stand within the limits of this Act, the owner of such carriage shall be liable to a penalty not exceeding five pounds for each time it is so found The driver also shall in every such case be liable to a like penalty unless he proves that he was ignorant of the fact of the carriage being an unlicensed carriage

Any hackney or stage carriage plying for hire, and any hackney carriage found on any stand without having such distinguishing mark, or being otherwise distinguished in such manner as may for the time being be prescribed by the said Secretary of State, shall be deemed to be an unlicensed carriage

Licensing Drivers of Hackney and Stage Carriages

Hackney carriage to be driven by licensed drivers

8 No hackney carriage shall ply for hire within the limits of this Act unless under the charge of a driver having a licence from the said Secretary of State, and no stage carriage shall ply for hire within the limits of this Act unless the conductor and driver of such carriage

have respectively licences from the said Secretary of State. If any hackney or stage carriage plies for hire in contravention of this section, the person driving the same, and also the owner of such carriage, unless he proves in the case of a hackney carriage that the driver, and in the case of a stage carriage that the conductor or driver, as the case may require, acted without his privity or consent, shall respectively be liable to a penalty not exceeding forty shillings

A licence to the driver or conductor of a hackney or stage carriage may be granted at such price, on such conditions, be in such form, be subject to revocation or suspension in such events, and generally be dealt with in such manner as the said Secretary of State may by order prescribe, subject to this provision, that any such licence shall, if not revoked or suspended, be in force for one year, and there shall be paid in respect thereof to the Receiver of the Metropolitan Police, to be carried to the account of the Metropolitan Police Fund, such sum not exceeding five shillings as the said Secretary of State may prescribe This clause shall not repeal the Tenth Section of an Act of the sixth and seventh years of the reign of Her present Majesty, chapter eighty six

Regulations relating to Hackney and Stage Carriages

9. The said Secretary of State may from time to time by order make regulations for all or any of the following purposes that is to say—

Regulations as to hackney and stage carriages.

(1) For regulating the number of persons to be carried in any hackney or stage carriage, and in what manner such number is to be shown on such carriage, and how such hackney carriages are to be furnished or fitted

(2) For fixing the stands of hackney carriages, and the distances to which they may be compelled to take passengers, and the persons to attend at such stands

(3) For fixing the rates or fares, as well for time as distance, to be paid for hackney carriages, and for securing the due publication of such fares provided that it shall not be made compulsory on the driver of any hackney carriage to take passengers at a less fare than the fare payable at the time of the passing of this Act

(4) For forming in the case of hackney carriages, a table of distances, as evidence for the purpose of any fare to be charged by distance, by the preparation of a book, map, or plan, or any combination of a book, map, or plan

(5) For securing the safe custody and re delivery of any property accidentally left in hackney or stage carriages and fixing the charges to be paid in respect thereof, with power to cause such property to be sold or to be given to the finder in the event of its not being claimed within a certain time

Subject to the following restrictions —

(1) In fixing the stands for hackney carriages within the City of London and the liberties thereof the consent of the Court of the Lord Mayor and Aldermen shall be required to any stand appointed by the Secretary of State

(2) No hackney carriage shall be compelled to take any passenger a greater distance for any one drive than six miles

(3) During such portion of time between sunset and sunrise as is from time to time prescribed, no driver shall ply for hire unless the hackney carriage under his charge be provided with a lamp properly trimmed and lighted, and fixed outside the carriage in such manner as is prescribed

This clause shall not repeal Section 13 of the Act of the fifth and sixth years of the reign of Her present Majesty, chapter seventy-nine, so far as regards existing carriages or any which may be built within one year after the passing of this Act

Penalties for breach of regulations
10. Where the Secretary of State is authorised to make any order under this Act, he may annex a penalty not exceeding forty shillings for the breach of such order or of any part or parts thereof, or of any regulation or regulations thereby made, and any penalties under this section shall be deemed to be penalties under this Act, and may be enforced accordingly

Licences by whom to be granted
11. Any licence grantable by a Secretary of State under this Act may, if the said Secretary of State so direct, be

granted by the Commissioner of the Metropolitan Police, or by such other person as the said Secretary of State appoints for the purpose

12. The said Secretary of State may appoint such officers and constables of the Metropolitan Police Force, and for the City of London of the City Police, as he thinks fit to perform any duties required to be performed for the purposes of carrying this Act into execution, and may award such sums by way of compensation for their services out of the moneys raised under this Act as he may think just. *(Powers to carry Act into execution.)*

Legal Proceedings and Miscellaneous

13. All penalties under this Act may be recovered summarily in the manner directed by the Act of the session of the eleventh and twelfth years of Her present Majesty, chapter forty-three, and any Act amending the same, and the term "justice" or "justice of the peace" shall include any metropolitan police magistrate sitting alone at a police court or other appointed place, and the Lord Mayor of the City of London or any alderman of the said city sitting alone or with others at the Mansion House or Guildhall *(Recovery of penalties.)*

14. The Commissioner of the Metropolitan Police may cause to be attached to any lamp post any placard or signal for the purpose of carrying into effect the provisions of this Act *(Placard &c may be affixed to lamp post.)*

15. All the provisions of the Acts relating to hackney carriages and metropolitan stage carriages in force at the time of the commencement of this Act shall, subject to any alteration made therein by this Act or by any order or regulation of the said Secretary of State made in pursuance of this Act, continue in force, and all such provisions of the said Acts as relate to licences granted under those Acts, or any of them, shall, subject to any alteration as aforesaid, apply to licences granted under this Act *(Existing Acts to continue in force)*

THE LONDON CAB ACT, 1896.
(59-60 V. 27.)

An Act to amend the Law relating to Cabs in London

[7th August, 1896.

Penalties for defrauding cabmen

1. If any person commits any of the following offences with respect to a cab namely—

    (a) Hires a cab, knowing or having reason to believe that he cannot pay the lawful fare, with intent to avoid payment of the lawful fare, or

    (b) Fraudulently endeavours to avoid payment of a fare lawfully due from him, or

    (c) Having failed or refused to pay a fare lawfully due from him, either refuses to give the driver an address at which he can be found, or, with intent to deceive, gives a false address,

    he shall be liable on summary conviction to pay, in addition to the lawful fare, a fine not exceeding forty shillings, or, in the discretion of the Court to be imprisoned for a term not exceeding fourteen days, and the whole or any part of any fine imposed may be applied in compensation to the driver

Repeal of 16 & 17 Vict. c 33.

2. Section 18 of The London Hackney Carriage Act, 1853, is hereby repealed from "and in case of any dispute" to the end of the section

Meaning of cab 32 & 33 Vict c 115

3. In this Act the expression "cab" shall mean any hackney carriage within the meaning of The Metropolitan Public Carriage Act, 1869

Short title

4. This Act may be cited as "The London Cab Act, 1896"

INDEX.

Absence from cab, 43.
Abstract of laws, 85
Abusive language, 38
Accident to horse or cab, 42.
Acts to be read together or not, 23, 30, 33, 35, 53 (*note* 2), 79
Address of driver, 90
Advertisements, 42
Agreement in writing, 87
Allowing another to drive, 40
Animals as luggage, 63
„ drawing cab, 9
„ injury to, 42
Appeal, 91
Armorial bearings, 79
Asquith Award, 104, 105.
Authorities, proceedings against, 91

"Back" fares, 37
Badge to be worn, 39
Bailor and bailee of cab, 68, 74.
Bicycles as luggage, 63.
"Bilker," 48
"Bilking" Act, 18, 48.
Bloomsbury Square, 14.
Blue Book, 7 *note*
Bodily harm through driving, 38
Books of distances, 54
Bound to be engaged, 16
Box, riding on, 38

INDEX

Cab, a necessary? Is a, 17.
    appointments of, 95, 96
  , construction of, 9, 95, 96
  ,, definition of, 9
  , in movement, 15
  , repairing &c., 42
  , standing still, 13, 15
  , unfit for use, 41
Cab and horse may be seized, 39, 40, 42, 81, 85
Carriers, cabmen as, 58
"Chairmarking," 80, 87
Change of address, 40
Character of driver, 82
Charing Cross, 53
Check string, 37
Children, 59, 60
City, the, 10, 11, 12, 43, 65.
Civil debt, 47, 48
Classes of cabs, 53
Commissioner of Police, 82, 86.
Committee of Enquiry, 6
Common informer, 32
Compensation, 39, 42, 44, 45, 46, 48, 71, 86, 87, 89
Complaint, 47
Concurrent jurisdictions, 51.
Conditional refusal to carry, 28.
Contract between proprietor and driver, 74, 104, 105
Contracts with Railway Company, 20, 21, 22
Corporations, powers of, 57.
Corpses, 26, 41
Costs, 31, 32, 33, 44, 45, 46, 48.
County Court remedy, 29, 48
County of London, 43, 56
Court for cab cases, 90

Court, payment into, 46.
Crawling, 13
Credit by cabman, 48
Croydon, 51
Cruelty to horse, 42, 81.

Damage by negligence, 38, 42, 43, 87
Defacement of licence, 40, 80, 88.
Default in payment of fine or costs, 33
Delivery of suppressed or revoked licence, 40
Demanding more than fare, 36, 37.
Deposit, 37, 59
Detaining badge, 40
    ,,   licence, 40
Dirty persons hiring, 17
Discretion of driver, 15
Disinfection, 27, 41
Distance, compulsory, 36
    ,,   hiring by, 53, 61
    ,,   how ascertained, 54.
Distances, books or tables of, 54.
Distress, 33, 34
Double hiring, 67
Driver away from cab, 43
    ,,   bailee of proprietor, 68, 94
    ,,   servant of proprietor, 66, 70, 71
    ,,   skill of, 82
Driver's scope of employment, 70
Drivers' licences, 82, 85
Drivers and proprietors, relation of, 85
Driving furiously, 38, 43
Drunken driver, 38, 39, 70
    ,,   persons hiring, 17
Duty on cabs, 75, 78, 79

Earnings of cab, 86, 87.
Employments, several, 88
Endorsement of licence, 89
Engaged already, 16.
Entering and quitting service, 79, 80, 88.
Examination of drivers, 82
Excise licence, 78, 79
Extra payments, 59

False pretences to get licence, 39
Fare a civil debt, 47.
    , beforehand, 27, 28
Fares, 52 to 58
    , anomalies of, 55
    ,, lowering of, 60
    ,, scales of, 30, 31, 53, 54.
    , ticket of, 41
Feeding horse in street, 38
Fines, 33, 87, 91
Furious driving, 38, 43

General Post Office, 14, 39, 53
Giving way to vehicles, 38
"Greenyard," 85

Hackney carriage, 9, 11 (see "Cab").
    , ,, Statutes, 106 to 154
Hansom, outside of, 63
    , luggage on, 94
Highway, offence in, 39
Hirer must take due care, 66, 67
Hiring, limitations of, 57
History of cabs, 1 to 7
    ,, ,, fares 52

Horse, attending to, 42.
," causing obstruction, 43
," safe or not, 69, 70
," tired, 17
," unfit for use, 41

Imprisonment, 33, 47, 87, 91
Infants, 17, 18.
Infectious diseases, 26, 27, 41
Information, 47.
Injury to persons or property, 38
Insane passengers, 17
Intoxicated driver, 38

Lamps, 64
Left, keeping to, 43
Legal complement, 41, 60, 95
Lending licence, 39
Licence, defacement of, 40, 80, 88.
," detaining, 40.
," driving without, 39
," endorsed, 35, 89
," plying without, 39
," procured by false pretences, 39
," renewal of, 83
," revoked, 35, 40
," suspended, 35, 40
," tampering with, 40.
," to be produced, 40.
Licences of drivers, 82
," restriction of numbers of, 84
Lighting, 64 to 66
Light locomotive, 9

"Limits" of the Act, 53.
" of the Metropolis, 53
Loitering, 38
London defined, 10 to 12
" County Council, regulation of, 65
" driver's knowledge of, 82
Loss of time, 45, 46
Lost or left property, 41, 48 to 50
Luggage, 37, 58, 62, 63
" charges, 37
" lost, 48 to 50, 66 to 74
" on hansom, 94

Magistrates, powers of, 86, 87.
Mandamus to Commissioner of Police, 83, 84.
Married woman, hiring by, 18
Means, proof of, 47, 48
Measuring wheel, 54
Messenger, cabman as, 58
Metropolis, 53
Metropolitan Police District, 10 to 12, 57, 92, 93
Middlesex, 11, 12
Mitigation of penalties, 34, 35.
More than number of passengers, 41
" " the legal fare, 28, 30, 31, 36
" " two passengers, 59
Motors, 9, 66, 96
" Order as to, 97 to 103.

Name and address of hirer, 31
Neglecting proprietor's notice, 40
Negligence of driver, 43, 66 to 74, 87.
Not bound to be hired, 19, 57.

Number of passengers, 36
    „   tampering with, 39
Numbered plates, 13, 39

Obstruction, 38, 43
"Offence," 48
Offences in streets, 38, 43
Omnibus, "privileged," 11
Order of Secretary of State, 32, 33, 75, 78, 83
    „   „   how far Clause 30 invalid, 50
"Outside" hansom, 63
Overcharge, 29.

Passengers by railway, 19, 23
    „   in unfit condition, 17
Passing vehicles, 43
Pedometer, 54.
Penal clause, extension of, 24
Penalties, 32 to 43, 87, 91
Person, injury to, 38, 42
Physical condition of cabs, 95, 96.
Placards, 42
"Place" in Statutes, 21, 25
Plates, 13, 39
Plumstead District, 56
Plying for hire, 13.
    „   improperly, 38
Police notices, 94 to 103
    „   regulations, 43
Private premises, 14
Privileged cabmen, 22, 32
    „   omnibus, 11
Procedure, 90, 91
Property, injury to, 38, 42

Proprietor a bailor, 68, 69, 71 to 74
,,   duties of, 74 to 81.
,,   not a common carrier, 66
,,   summoned to produce driver, 86
Proprietor's licence, 38, 41, 75, 78.
,,   responsibility for driver, 66
Proprietors and drivers, relation of, 85
Public place, 15, 20 to 22, 25
"Put into" the cab, 19

Quarter Sessions, 21

Racing, 38
Radius, 53, 56
Railway cabs, 19 to 25, 57
,,   stations, cabs at, 25, 26
,,   companies, contracts of, 21, 22, 57, 58
,,   Commissioners' powers, 25
Reasonable excuse, 16, 17, 28
Refusing to be hired, 36
,,   ,, pay, 18, 31
,,   ,, take luggage, 37
Registrar of Metropolitan Public Carriages, 82
Remedies of both parties, 28 *et seq.*
,,   ,, the driver, 45 to 51
,,   ,, the hirer, 28 to 44
Report, 7 (*note*)
Reward in case of lost property, 49
Right to hire, 16
Road up, 54
Route, 43

Scale of fares, more than one, 53, 54
Scope of employment, 70
Servant a passenger, 19

Special contracts, 16, 19, 57
Speed, 10, 41, 61
Standing improperly, 38
    „   still, 13
Standings, 13, 14, 38
    „   at railway stations, 19
Stating a case, 91
Statistics, 6, 7
Statutes, 106 to 154.
Strangers riding, 37, 38
Streets, offences in, 38, 39.
Summary Jurisdiction Act, 33, 34, 46, 47
Summons, procedure as to, 31, 32, 46, 90
Sunday, 58

Taxes on cabs, 78, 79
Ticket of driver, 41, 85
Time, compulsory, 36.
    „ hiring by, 53, 56, 61
    „   „   „ not always compulsory 52.
Tips, 36 (*note 1*).
Transferring licence, 39
Trespassers, 16, 24
Two horse cabs, 52

Unable to pay fare, 17, 26
Unattended cab, 39
Unlicensed cab, 14, 15, 23, 39

Vestries, 14

Wages of driver, 86
Waiting, 37, 58
Warrant, 45, 90, 91
Wheel, measuring, 54

JORDAN & SONS, LIMITED,

INCORPORATION OF COMPANIES &c.

JORDAN & SONS, LIMITED, will be happy to render assistance in all matters connected with the Formation, Management, and Winding Up of Public Companies. The large practical experience of the Directors in business of this nature frequently enables them to be of service to Solicitors and others who entrust them with the supervision and printing of Prospectuses, Memorandums and Articles of Association, Contracts, Special Resolutions, Notices, and other Documents.

All papers put into their hands are printed with the utmost care and expedition, and in conformity with the requirements of the Companies Acts and the Registrar of Joint Stock Companies

MEMORANDUMS AND ARTICLES OF ASSOCIATION

and other Documents sent to them to be Stamped and Registered are immediately attended to, and the Certificates of Incorporation obtained and forwarded as soon as issued

STAMPING DEEDS AND OTHER DOCUMENTS.

JORDAN & SONS, LIMITED, give particular attention to the proper Stamping of Agreements, Deeds, and other Instruments All documents forwarded to them for that purpose are carefully examined, and, if necessary, submitted for adjudication as to the Duty chargeable thereon

120 Chancery Lane, and 8 Bell Yard, London, W.C.

A List of New Law Books and New Editions

PUBLISHED BY

JORDAN & SONS, LIMITED.

Twenty-first Edition, Price 5s net; by Post 5s 6d

A HANDY BOOK on the FORMATION, MANAGEMENT, and WINDING UP of JOINT STOCK COMPANIES. By WILLIAM JORDAN, Registration and Parliamentary Agent, and F. GORE-BROWNE, M A, of the Inner Temple, Barrister-at-law

"The style is easy and perspicuous, and we should imagine that it is just the book which every Secretary of a company would like to have constantly ready at hand as a guide in all cases of difficulty arising in the management of the affairs of his undertaking"—*Law Journal*

"This is the Twenty-first Edition of this most useful of Manuals on Company Law, which has been in constant demand since first issued by Messrs JORDAN A number of important legal decisions have been pronounced since the Twentieth Edition was published in February, 1897, and the Editors have carefully revised the work in the light of those judgments The volume has grown in bulk a little, but it still deserves its title. We consider that no conscientious Company Secretary can afford to do without the book, while it is almost equally indispensable to Solicitors, Directors, Promoters, Liquidators, Auditors, and others."—*Investors' Guardian*

JORDAN & SONS, LIMITED,

In Preparation Second Edition   Price 18s., by Post 18s. 6d

CONCISE PRECEDENTS UNDER THE COMPANIES ACTS. Containing numerous Precedents of Memorandums and Articles of Association; Agreements with Vendors, and other Preliminary Contracts; Underwriting Letters, Commission Notes, &c., Forms of Debentures and Trust Deeds, Schemes of Winding Up and Reconstruction of Companies and Arrangements with Creditors, Forms of Resolutions and Petitions, Notices of Motion and Summons, Pleadings in Actions, &c. By F. GORE-BROWNE, M.A., Barrister-at-Law, Joint Author of "A Handy Book on the Formation, Management, and Winding Up of Companies."

"This book aims at supplying a real business want by providing such short and clear forms as are constantly being required by both lawyers and laymen who have to do with the Formation, the Management, and the Winding up of Companies The Author has, by way of introductory remarks to each chapter and numerous notes throughout, kept his object clearly in view, and explained everywhere all practical points as they arise, with the addition of useful hints, which are evidently the outcome of experience."—*Manchester Guardian*

THE STANDARD WORK ON THE STAMP LAWS.

Sixth Edition, Price 6s net, by Post 6s. 6d.

THE LAW OF STAMP DUTIES ON DEEDS AND OTHER INSTRUMENTS. Containing The Stamp Act 1891, The Stamp Duties Management Act 1891, and Acts Amending the same; a Summary of Case Law, Notes of Practice and Administration; Tables of Exemptions, **the Old and New Death Duties;** and the Excise Licence Duties. By E N. ALPE, of the Middle Temple, Barrister-at-Law, and the Solicitor's Department, Inland Revenue

This Edition has been revised and brought down to date. It contains all the alterations relating to Stamp Duties that have been effected by the various Inland Revenue and other Acts passed since 1891, and the provisions relating to the Estate, Excise, and Stamp Duties contained in The Finance Acts, 1894 to 1897.

120 Chancery Lane, and 8 Bell Yard, London, W.C.

JORDAN & SONS, LIMITED,

Fifth Edition, Price 5s net, by Post 5s 6d

THE SECRETARY'S MANUAL ON THE LAW AND PRACTICE OF JOINT STOCK COMPANIES, with Forms and Precedents. By JAMES FITZPATRICK, Fellow of the Institute of Chartered Accountants, and V DE S FOWKE, Barrister-at-Law

"This is the best book of the sort that we have yet seen It explains the duties and responsibilities of a Secretary from the commencement The various books that are required are set out in detail, and every act in the life of a Company, until its winding up, is described"—*Financial News*

Second Edition, Price 5s net, by Post 5s 6d

THE COMPANIES ACTS, 1862 to 1898; The Life Assurance Companies Acts, 1870 to 1872, and The Life Assurance Companies (Payment into Court) Act, 1896; The Forged Transfers Acts, 1891 and 1892; The Stannaries Acts, 1869 and 1887, and The Stannaries Court Abolition Act, 1896; The Preferential Payments in Bankruptcy Amendment Act, 1897; and other Statutes and Statutory Enactments relating to or affecting Joint Stock Companies formed under the Companies Acts, with Cross References and a full Analytical Index. By V. DE S FOWKE, of Lincoln's Inn, Barrister-at-Law.

BY THE SAME AUTHOR *Price 6s. net; by Post 6s 6d*

THE INDUSTRIAL AND PROVIDENT SOCIETIES ACTS, 1893 and 1894. With a History of the Legislation dealing with Industrial and Provident Societies, the Text of the Acts with Notes, the Treasury Regulations, 1894, Sets of Model Rules, Numerous Forms, and a Complete Index.

"An excellent handbook, dealing with the provisions of The Industrial and Provident Societies Acts, 1893 and 1894 The Author has added sets of Model Rules and numerous practical Forms A vast section of the population is interested in societies of this class, and to those—be they lawyers or laymen—who form and work them we commend this book as a most serviceable guide"—*The Brief*

120 Chancery Lane, and 8 Bell Yard, London, W.C.

JORDAN & SONS, LIMITED,

IMPORTANT WORK ON THE LAW OF TRUSTS.

Second Edition, Price 12s 6d. net, by Post 13s

THE LAW OF TRUSTS AND TRUSTEES under The Trustee Act 1888, The Trust Investment Act 1889, The Trustee Act 1893, The Trustee Act 1893 Amendment Act 1894, and The Judicial Trustees Act 1896, with Explanatory Notes; the Rules of Court under The Trustee Act 1893 and The Judicial Trustees Act 1896, a full List of Trust Investments, numerous Forms, references to all the recent decisions on the Acts, and a complete Index. By ARTHUR REGINALD RUDALL and JAMES WILLIAM GREIG, Barristers-at-Law

"Of the books dealing with the Law of Trusts this is certainly one of the best and most complete."—*Manchester Guardian*

BY THE SAME AUTHORS. *Price 10s net, by Post 10s 6d*

THE LAW AS TO COPYHOLD ENFRANCHISEMENT UNDER THE COPYHOLD ACT, 1894. Containing the Text of the Act with Explanatory Notes, Comparative Tables of Repealed Statutes, Minutes of the Board of Agriculture, Scales of Compensation, numerous Forms, and a full Analytical Index.

A notable feature of this work is the large number of Forms, which have been prepared to meet almost every contingency that can arise in connection with the Enfranchisement of Copyholds.

BY THE SAME AUTHORS. *Price 5s. net; by Post 5s 6d.*

THE LAW OF LAND TRANSFER by Registration of Title under The Land Transfer Acts, 1875 and 1897. Containing an Introductory Chapter, the Full Text of the Acts with Explanatory Notes, the Land Transfer Rules, 1898, with the Subsidiary Rules and Orders, Table of Fees, and a Complete Index.

120 Chancery Lane, and 8 Bell Yard, London, W.C.

JORDAN & SONS, LIMITED,

Bound in Boards with Leather Back, 2s 6d ; in Cloth Boards, gilt lettered 3s 6d   By Post 6d extra

THE COMPANIES' DIARY AND AGENDA BOOK for 1899.
This Diary is compiled mainly for the use of Secretaries, Directors, and other Company Officials, and contains a large amount of special information relative to their duties and responsibilities, together with much other general information on questions of daily occurrence

The book is of foolscap folio size, the Diary having a full page for each week. A few pages, specially ruled, are provided for Memoranda and Reminders of a permanent nature, and a quire of good ruled foolscap for Agenda, Rough Minutes of Proceedings at Board and General Meetings, or for use as a Note or Record Book at other times as may be required, is also included

Fourth Edition, Price 10s. net, by Post 10s 6d

NOTES on PERUSING TITLES.
Containing Observations on the Points most frequently arising on a Perusal of Titles to Real and Leasehold Property, and an Epitome of the Notes arranged by way of Reminders, being an attempt to Reduce the Perusal of Abstracts to a System   With an Appendix on the Appointment of a Real Representative by The Land Transfer Act, 1897   By LEWIS E EMMET, Solicitor

"The extraordinary success of this book—it has run to four editions in three and-a-half years—is its own best recommendation   Nor has this success been undeserved   We have had occasion to speak highly of previous editions, and we may say of this that it is in every respect admirable ; there is no book on the subject which we can so confidently recommend   The Author is obviously thoroughly conversant with what he is writing about and the literature relating thereto, and what is so important in a branch of law where modern rules are of supreme value, he is above all up to date"—*Law Notes*

Price 6d , by Post 7d

THE A1 SHORTHAND FOR VERBATIM REPORTING Without the Aid of a Master.
By LEWIS E EMMET

---

120 Chancery Lane, and 8 Bell Yard, London, W.C.

JORDAN & SONS, LIMITED,

Price 15s., for Cash with Order 12s. 6d., by Post 6d. extra

A PRACTICAL TREATISE ON PATENTS, TRADE MARKS, AND DESIGNS. With a Digest of Colonial and Foreign Patent Laws; the Text of The Patents, Designs, and Trade Marks Acts, 1883 to 1888 (Consolidated); the Rules, Fees, and Forms relating to Patents, Designs, and Trade Marks (Consolidated); the International Convention for the Protection of Industrial Property; Precedents of Agreements, Assignments, Licences, Mortgages, &c., and a full Analytical Index. By DAVID FULTON, A.M.I.C.E., Fellow of the Chartered Institute of Patent Agents, and of the Middle Temple, Barrister-at-Law.

"There is always room for a good book, and we have no hesitation in saying that Mr. FULTON's treatise belongs to that category. The style is clear, the text is not overlaid with decisions, and everything is inserted which the lay reader needs to know. The book contains one admirable feature which should commend it to students.—In the tabulated list of cases cited a short note is appended to each, stating the essential point or points affected by the decision."—*Glasgow Herald.*

Second Edition, Price 3s. 6d. net, by Post 3s. 9d.

PROVISIONAL ORDERS OF THE BOARD OF TRADE in reference to Gas and Water, Tramway, Pier and Harbour, and Electric Light Undertakings. A Manual of Practice for Promoters, Opponents, and Others. By FRANCIS J. CROWTHER, Parliamentary Agent.

"Local authorities anxious to secure Provisional Orders of whatever nature, whether they apply to gas, water, tramway, pier and harbour, or electric lighting undertakings, will find in Mr. CROWTHER's handbook on 'Provisional Orders of the Board of Trade' an invaluable guide. Mr. CROWTHER's experience as a Parliamentary Agent befits him to speak on the subject with which he deals, and whether we want Provisional Orders, or are anxious to oppose, Mr. CROWTHER's book lucidly sets forth the procedure to be observed."—*Local Government Journal.*

120 Chancery Lane, and 8 Bell Yard, London, W.C.

JORDAN & SONS, LIMITED,

Price 20s. net, by Post 6d extra

THE LAW OF BILLS OF SALE. Containing a General Introduction in Ten Chapters; the Text of the Repealed Statutes; The Bills of Sale Acts, 1878 to 1891, with Notes, and an Appendix of Forms. By JAMES WEIR, M.A., Barrister-at-Law

"One of the best law books of recent years. Not merely does it seem destined to take its place with practitioners as the leading authority on the subject, but it is a contribution of real and permanent value to legal literature."—*Saturday Review*

Price 1s each, or 10s per dozen, Post free

TABLE A OF THE COMPANIES ACT, 1862. With Explanatory Notes and Comments, the Rules of the London Stock Exchange relating to Shares and Stocks, Miscellaneous Provisions of the Companies Acts, Tables of Stamp Duties and Fees on Registering Companies, The Memorandum of Association Act 1890, The Directors' Liability Act 1890, The Companies Act, 1898, and other information.

This book is intended to supply the Officials and Shareholders of the numerous Companies registered under Table A with a copy of the Regulations under which they are governed, with such Explanatory Notes and Comments as experience has shown to be frequently needed. The book is of a convenient size for the desk or the pocket, and, besides its utility for general reference, will be found of assistance at Meetings of Directors and Shareholders in determining questions relating to Transfers, Forfeiture of Shares, Voting Powers, and other matters

Price 3s 6d net, by Post 3s 9d

REMINDERS ON COMPANY LAW. With Hints as to Drafting all Forms in General Use and Advising on Matters connected with Joint Stock Companies. By V DE S FOWKE, of Lincoln's Inn, Barrister-at-Law, Joint Author of "The Secretary's Manual on the Law and Practice of Joint Stock Companies"

120 Chancery Lane, and 8 Bell Yard, London, W.C.

JORDAN & SONS, LIMITED,

Third Edition, Price 7s. 6d net; by Post 8s.

THE PARISH COUNCILLOR'S GUIDE TO THE LOCAL GOVERNMENT ACT, 1894, with Introductory Chapters as follows —The Parish Meeting; Procedure at the Parish Meeting and the Parish Poll; The Parish Council and its Constitution, Powers and Duties of the Parish Council, The Affairs of the Church and Ecclesiastical Charities· Schools; The Vestry, Boards of Guardians and District Councils; Parish Lands and Allotments; Elections, Financial Provisions Rates Loans, London and the Act. By H C RICHARDS, M.P, and J P H SOPER, Barristers-at-Law.

By the same Authors   *Price 3s 6d. net; by Post 4s*

THE LOCAL GOVERNMENT ACT, 1894. Containing the full Text of the Act with Explanatory Notes, the Incorporated Sections of The Public Health Act, 1875; The Allotments Acts, 1887 and 1890, and Circulars of the Local Government Board and the Charity Commissioners

Second Edition, Price 2s 6d. net, by Post 2s 9d

THE CANDIDATES' AND AGENTS' GUIDE IN CONTESTED ELECTIONS. A Complete *Vade Mecum* for Candidates, Agents, and Workers in Parliamentary and Municipal Contests By H. C. RICHARDS, M P, Barrister-at-Law

By the same Author   *Price 2s 6d net, by Post 2s 9d*

THE CORRUPT AND ILLEGAL PRACTICES PREVENTION ACT, 1883, Annotated and Explained, with Notes of Judicial Decisions in Cases of Bribery, Treating, Undue Influence, Impersonation, &c., and a Copious Index

---

120 Chancery Lane, and 8 Bell Yard, London, W.C.

JORDAN & SONS, LIMITED,

Price 5s net, by Post 5s. 6d.

THE BENEFICES ACT and Ecclesiastical Proceedings under the various Statutes relating to the Discipline of the Clergy, and Generally. With Introductory Notes on Transfer of Rights of Patronage, Institution and Inhibition, Rules of Procedure and Sequestration, and Miscellaneous Provisions under the Act, Chapters on Ecclesiastical Offences, Faculties, the Ecclesiastical Courts, and Recent Decisions in Ecclesiastical Matters; and an Appendix containing the full text of The Benefices Act 1898, and the Benefices Rules, 1898 and 1899, The Church Discipline Act 1840, and The Clergy Discipline Act 1892, and the Rules and Forms under that Act. By HAROLD HARDY, B.A., Barrister-at-Law

Price 3s. 6d net, by Post 3s 9d.

THE LAW OF COPYRIGHT. Containing Chapters on the History of Literary Copyright, Unpublished Works, Literary Copyright by Statute, Dramatic and Musical Copyright, Engravings, Paintings, Drawings, Photographs, and Sculpture, and International and Colonial Copyright, an Appendix of Statutes, the Order in Council of 1887, the Text of the Berne Convention, the American Act of 1891, and a full Index. By B A COHEN, Barrister-at-Law

Price 5s net, by Post 5s 6d

A MANUAL OF THE LAW OF CONTRACT for the USE OF STUDENTS. By J G COLCLOUGH, B A, of the King's Inn, Dublin, and M MAJID ULLAH, of the Middle Temple, Barrister-at-Law

This Abridgment of the Law of Contract is published for the purpose of meeting the requirement of Law Students for a shorter, more compact, and more accessible treatise on the subject than has hitherto been published, the great objection to previous works on the Law of Contract being their bulk and price. The subject is dealt with clearly and succinctly, and yet completely

120 Chancery Lane, and 8 Bell Yard, London, W C.

JORDAN & SONS, LIMITED,

Price 25s net; by Post 25s. 6d

AMERICAN CORPORATION LEGAL MANUAL for 1899. A compilation of the essential features of the Statutory Law regulating the Formation, Management, and Dissolution of General Business Corporations in America (North, Central, and South) and other Countries of the World, with Special Digests of the United States Street Railway Laws and the Laws of Building and Loan Associations, Treatise on Receiverships, and Synopses of the Patent, Trade Mark, and Copyright Laws of the World. Edited by CHARLES L. BORGMEYER, Member of the New Jersey Bar, Newark, N.J.

(JORDAN & SONS, Limited, are the English Publishers of and Sole Agents for this Book.)

Price 25s., for Cash with Order 20s.; by Post 9d. extra.

THE STOCK EXCHANGE YEAR-BOOK for 1899. A careful digest of information relating to the origin, history, and present position of each of the Public Securities and Joint Stock Companies known to the Markets of the United Kingdom. By THOMAS SKINNER.

Price 15s., Post free on receipt of remittance

THE MINING MANUAL for 1899. Contains full particulars of all Mining Companies known to the Exchanges of London and the Provinces, together with a List of Mining Directors. By WALTER R. SKINNER.

Price 3s 6d net, by Post 3s 9d

BOOK-KEEPING for Terminating Building Societies. Illustrated by a Year's Transactions of a Society, with a Statement of Accounts and a Balance Sheet, and a Short Chapter on Auditing. By JOHN FREDERICK LEES, Accountant.

120 Chancery Lane, and 8 Bell Yard, London, W.C.

JORDAN & SONS, LIMITED,

Trade Marks AND Designs Registered.

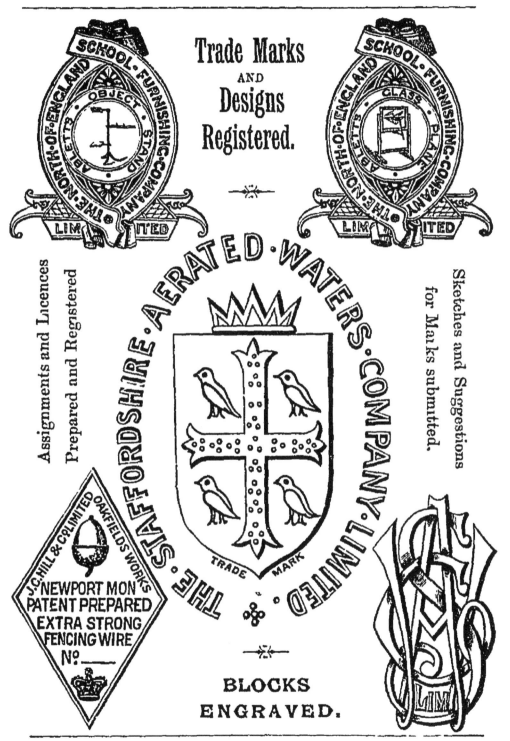

Assignments and Licences Prepared and Registered

Sketches and Suggestions for Marks submitted.

BLOCKS ENGRAVED.

120 Chancery Lane, and 8 Bell Yard, London, W.C.

JORDAN & SONS, LIMITED,

CORPORATE and COMPANY SEALS.

JORDAN & SONS, LIMITED, are noted for the high quality and artistic design of the Corporate and other Seals designed and engraved by them.

In consequence of their special facilities for the rapid execution of this branch of Art, they are enabled to supply Seals where necessary at exceedingly short notice.

Japanned Cases for the safe custody of Seals, with two good lever locks and duplicate keys, 12/6, 15/-, and 17/6, according to size of Press.

Mahogany case, with two patent locks and duplicate keys, 30/-

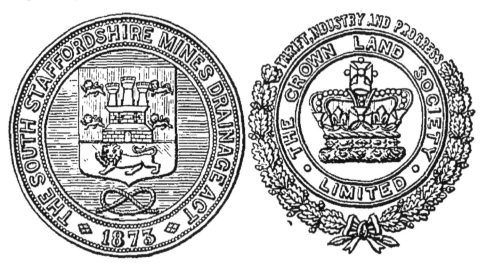

SKETCHES AND ESTIMATES FREE.

120 Chancery Lane, and 8 Bell Yard, London, W.C.

JORDAN & SONS, LIMITED,

Specimens of Seals designed and engraved by Jordan & Sons, Limited.

120 Chancery Lane, and 8 Bell Yard, London, W.C.

JORDAN & SONS, LIMITED,

COMMON SEAL
Engraved and Fitted to Screw Press,
SIMILAR TO THIS
From £5 5s.

COMMON SEAL
Engraved and Fitted to Lever Press,
SIMILAR TO THIS
From 21s.

➤✳:✳◀

These Seals may be secured with Padlocks or Clamps fitted to the Press, or may be placed in Cases fitted with Two or more Locks.

➤✳:✳◀

COMMON SEAL
Engraved and Fitted to Lever Press,
SIMILAR TO THIS
From 40s.

120 Chancery Lane, and 8 Bell Yard, London, W.C.

JORDAN & SONS, LIMITED,

JAPANNED CASES
For Corporate and Company Seals

These Cases are for the purpose of securing the Seals of Corporations and Companies from use by unauthorised persons, to keep the Seals free from dust, and to enable them to be easily carried from place to place. The Cases are fitted with two good lever locks, with duplicate keys to each, and are stocked in three sizes, at the following prices —

No 1	No. 2	No 3
(9 by 6¾ by 4¼ ins)	(10¼ by 8¼ by 4¾ ins)	(11¼ by 9 by 5¼ ins)
12/6	**15/-**	**15/-**

Other sizes made to order

Lettering Case with name of Corporation or Company involves a small extra charge, according to length of name

---

120 Chancery Lane, and 8 Bell Yard, London, W.C.

JORDAN & SONS,

LIMITED,

Make a Speciality of Printing Memorandums and Articles of Association, Prospectuses, Trust Deeds, Agreements, Minutes of Evidence, Provisional Orders, Petitions, &c., and Legal, Parliamentary, and Company work of all kinds.

Estimates given for the Printing and Publication of Legal and Scientific Works, and Books in General Literature.

JORDAN & SONS, LIMITED, are in daily attendance at the Companies' Registration Office, the Inland Revenue Department, the Bills of Sale Office, Stationers' Hall, the Registry of Wills, the Legacy and Succession Duty Offices, and the Registries of Births, Marriages, and Deaths, and give immediate attention to all matters entrusted to them in connection with those Departments.

---

120 CHANCERY LANE, LONDON.

Lightning Source UK Ltd.
Milton Keynes UK
UKHW030856291122
413053UK00009B/387